The Love Covenant

The Love Covenant

Preparing for Your
Wedding Ceremony
or
Your Anniversary Celebration

ST. PAUL EDITIONS

NIHIL OBSTAT:
Rev. Richard V. Lawlor, S.J.
Censor

IMPRIMATUR:
✠ Humberto Cardinal Medeiros
Archbishop of Boston

Catechesis on the Sacrament of Matrimony by the Daughters of St. Paul.

Photo credits:
A. Alvarez 34, 90; Ciambrone 109; DSP cover; Hawkins 55; Romano 47

ISBN 0-8198-4432-2 cloth
     0-8198-4433-0 paper

Copyright © 1983, by the Daughters of St. Paul

Printed in the U.S.A., by the Daughters of St. Paul
50 St. Paul's Ave., Boston, MA 02130

The Daughters of St. Paul are an international congregation of religious women serving the Church with the communications media.

CONTENTS

Preface

Are you beginning to make plans for your marriage, your wedding or anniversary? *The Love Covenant* is designed to help you.

Some sections of *The Love Covenant* will help you with the spiritual preparation; other sections will provide for the practical aspects.

You may wish to begin by reading this entire book before devoting more time to a particular part of it. By using the table of contents on page 9, you will be able to locate specific aspects involved in your preparation.

By filling in the checklists on pages 115 to 132, you will note the progress made and the decisions reached for your wedding day.

In all, *The Love Covenant* helps you to *prepare* in a particular way for that special first day that begins your personal love covenant for life with one another.

In the sacrament of marriage,
a man and a woman—
who at Baptism became members of Christ
and hence have the duty of manifesting
Christ's attitudes in their lives
—are assured of the help they need
to develop their love
in a faithful and indissoluble union,
and to respond with generosity
to the gift of parenthood.
As the Second Vatican Council declared:
Through this sacrament,
Christ Himself becomes present
in the life of the married couple
and accompanies them,
so that they may love each other
and their children,
just as Christ loved His Church
by giving Himself up for her
(cf. Gaudium et spes, no. 48;
cf. Eph. 5:25).

Pope John Paul II

PREPARING FOR YOUR WEDDING

PRELIMINARY REFLECTIONS
THE BRIDE'S PRAYER
THE GROOM'S PRAYER
CONSULTATIONS AND DECISIONS
REHEARSAL

Preliminary Reflections

...ON THE LOVE COVENANT

From the beginning of the human race, family life has been part of God's plan for man. The Bible tells us that He told our first parents:

"Be fruitful, multiply,
fill the earth and conquer it" (Genesis 1:28).**

Marriage is a *covenant*—a lasting agreement of deep and true friendship. You might compare it to the covenant between God and the Chosen People of Old Testament times or between Jesus and His Church now. Marriage means sharing and caring, and it is meant to lead to deep happiness.

According to God's plan, marriage always has two purposes. These cannot be separated. One purpose of marriage is to bring children into the world and raise them well. The other is to love one another with a real, self-sacrificing, lifelong love that helps husband and wife to grow as persons and become holy.

Parents should lovingly welcome as God's most precious gifts the children that He will give them. They should also love and help one another for a life-

time, because by divine will marriage is for life. Jesus made that clear when he said:

"Let no man separate what God has joined.... Whoever divorces his wife and marries another is guilty of adultery against her. And if a woman divorces her husband and marries another she is guilty of adultery too" (Mk. 10:9, 11-12).**

God made marriage unbreakable for the good of yourselves, your children, and society It is important for you as young people to keep this in mind when you think of getting married, in order to make a wise choice of a life partner.

Besides knowing that marriage is for life and what its purposes are, as a couple you should also know yourselves and one another well before marriage. Ask yourselves: Do we have enough in common? Can we really get along well? Are we ready to make sacrifices for one another and for our children?

As young persons, you can become even more sure that you are making a wise choice by praying for God's guidance and asking advice from your parents and the priest to whom you usually go for confession.

In preparing for marriage you will want to learn about the beauty, nobility and duties of married life. It would be a wise choice to practice the virtues, especially chastity, and receive Penance and the Holy Eucharist often.

...ON THE SACRAMENT OF MATRIMONY

Matrimony is conferred when a baptized man and a baptized woman express their mutual consent under conditions established or permitted by the

Church. The bride and groom, therefore, confer the sacrament on one another.

Jesus raised marriage to the dignity of a sacrament because the vocation to the married state demands much virtue. By the sacrament of Matrimony, you will receive strength for fulfilling your obligations to one another and your children. Through it you will be filled with the Spirit of Christ who permeates your lives with faith, hope and love. Because of it as Christian spouses you walk together towards heaven and endeavor to grow in perfection and holiness.

Although Catholics may receive permission to marry non-Catholics, this should not be encouraged. During the difficult times that come in life for everyone, sharing the same Faith will help you very much.

In mixed marriages, the Catholic husband or wife—the Church teaches—has to take care to strengthen his or her faith, to continually give the non-Catholic partner a shining example, and to rear all the children in the Catholic Faith.

The *sign* of the sacrament of Matrimony is made up of words only—the *vows* or promises by which you, the bride and groom, declare that you are marrying one another. To show this more clearly, you may join hands or exchange rings, but these actions are not necessary for the sacrament.

There are many ways that the marriage vows (promises) may be worded, but the meaning of them is this: You promise to love and be loyal to one another in good times and bad times, in sickness and in health all the days of your lives until death separates you.

When as a Christian couple you marry, you give the sacrament to one another. The priest is present to give you the Church's blessing in God's name and to remind you both of your responsibilities to one another and to the children God will send you.

What does the Lord Jesus do for you who have joined yourselves together in Matrimony? He gives you His Spirit to make you both holier by growth in grace. He also gives you the help you will need to love one another loyally for life and raise your children as good Catholics and citizens.

...ON THE "LITTLE CHURCH"

The family is the first school, in which your children will learn how to live and work with others in love and respect. When your children will receive love and good training, they will become ready to face life with confidence and a sense of responsibility regarding the salvation, happiness and progress of their fellow men. They will become good citizens. When families are strong, nations are strong.

The *Christian* family is a "little Church." From you, your children will learn how very important God and religion are in life. They will learn that God loves all men and that therefore they are to be good and kind to everyone, without discrimination. Plan to teach your children to pray and always to trust God as a loving father, and they will grow up happy, knowing that their lives have a meaning and a purpose for their good and the good of others. From the family of today come the new families, and priests, brothers, and sisters of tomorrow.

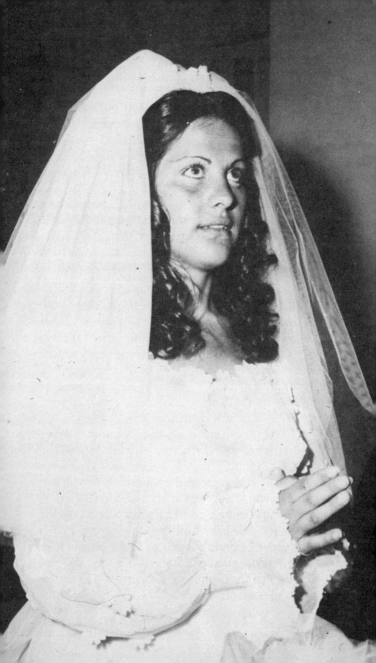

The Bride's Prayer

Lord, grant that I may be worthy of him who has chosen me to be his bride and whom I have chosen to be my husband. Lord, grant that I may correspond to the trust of his name and provide for the needs of his house. Lord, grant that I may repay his love with a lifetime of faithfulness.

Because we shall be companions throughout life, give me the strength to walk at his side for the whole length of the way. And because he has selected me as the sister of his destiny, make me the sharer of all his hours of fatigue and happiness, but reserve for me the greater part of every pain. Because he has chosen me as the mother of his children, infuse in my soul the necessary strength to be always the support, the joy and the peace of our home.

Thus may I become for him the smile and the hope, the refuge and the certainty in the routine of our daily life. In our home today, tomorrow and always, render me worthy of my position as friend, wife and mother. In every hour of sunshine and storm, grant that I may always work for the happiness of him whom I love. Amen.

The Groom's Prayer

My God, on this great day I kneel before You at the dawn of a new life.

I tremble...when faced with the realization of the lofty commitment which I take upon myself. Ahead of me lies a life of love joined to the woman I have chosen. I pledge to You fidelity, devotion and service to her and to the children You will send us. By myself I am not capable of this honored task but Your help and grace will conquer all.

Never as today have I felt Your divine presence. I need Your presence. Make me the man You expect me to be. Mold me into another Joseph. Make me resemble that silent and just Husband of Mary. Give me a pure love and noble sentiments, a love as true as Adam and Eve's before sin tainted paradise.

Give me a love for her which extends far beyond myself, which is not limited or measured by days, weeks and years. May it never fade when age and infirmities rob us of youth. Give us both an understanding of higher things; and make that knowledge blossom into wisdom.

In joy, in sorrow, in triumph, in failure, I choose this woman for my queen, my friend, my support, my other self, until death, and even beyond...for death will not quench my love.

Bless our home with Your sacred presence. Give us the joy which You left with that unknown couple at Cana in Galilee. Two lives this day are knitted into one. Together we will love and cherish the family you send us. Together we will present ourselves to You at the journey's end. Make us, O my God, the couple You expect us to be. Walk with us through life and heaven will begin right here on earth. Thank You for creating the woman I love; thank You for giving her to me. Amen.

Consultations and Decisions

Since you are looking forward to a lifetime of love together as husband and wife, you will want to prepare in the best way possible not only for your wedding day but for your marriage. That is why months before the wedding—sometimes three, possibly even six months, depending on diocesan guidelines—you should notify your pastor of your intention to marry each other. Normally the pastor to be consulted will be that of the bride's parish, but for a just reason it may also be that of the groom's. The priest or deacon who will assist you during this preparatory time will inform you of programs for the engaged, and he will want you to plan with him the wedding liturgy.

While planning the major and minor aspects of your wedding day, you will want to benefit by discussing matters with your parents, with other couples, even your friends who have recently married, or aunts and uncles who share with you their fond memories.

Some family members and close friends will offer to help with certain aspects of the day's events; others will be delighted to accept if you invite them to help or participate. Whatever help another gives in preparation for the wedding or on the day itself may even take the place of the usual wedding gift. In fact, both giver and receiver may prefer such an arrangement.

On your wedding day, the marriage bond will unite you and your spouse together in a lifetime covenant of love; it will also bring together two "extended families": parents, grandparents, brothers and sisters, aunts and uncles, cousins, nieces and nephews.

Your gracious invitation to each one to participate will make your celebration of the sacrament of Matrimony memorable, not just for yourselves, but for all those who will share your joy on this day.

You may desire to have a theme around which to plan your wedding. A theme will help you select the biblical readings and hymns, as well as prepare the General Intercessions (Prayer of the Faithful) and possibly even a banner for the lectern or altar or for the reception hall.

A theme will be easy to decide upon after reading over the prayers of the wedding rite itself and the wealth of biblical readings provided to choose from: e.g., *Our Covenant of Love* (from Old Testament Reading 8); *Love Never Fails* (from New Testament Reading 4); *God Is With Us* (from New Testament Reading 8); *Let Us Rejoice and Be Glad* (from New Testament Reading 10); *The Kindness of the Lord Is from Eternity to Eternity* (from Responsorial Psalm 3); *Let Your Light Shine* (from Gospel 2); *Love One Another As I Have Loved You* (from Gospel 8); *Love Is Our Constant Calling* (from Preface 3); *Faithful in Love* (from Nuptial Blessing 2).

Your choices will reflect the deep commitment of your faith-heritage.

After considering the spiritual atmosphere of your wedding day, you will need to determine more practical points:

—when will the date of the wedding be? the rehearsal?

—whether your wedding will be in a formal or informal atmosphere (the invitations you choose will set the tone)

—how much money you can afford to spend

—how many people you want to invite

—who will pay for the wedding? for the reception?

(Although it is customary that the bride's parents pay for the wedding and the reception and the groom for the honeymoon, the groom's family may offer to pay for the reception, and at times, you yourselves if you are both working may wish to pay for some of your own expenses)

—whether a wedding booklet will be purchased or prepared

—which hymns are most appropriate in reflecting your theme.

These are just some points at random. The detailed checklists on pages 115 to 132 will help you plan both major and minor aspects of your wedding day. Then, on the day itself, you and all who participate will relax and enjoy those precious moments.

Rehearsal

An evening or two before your wedding day, you will want to have a rehearsal of the ceremony at the church. Everyone involved should be notified well in advance of date and time scheduled by your pastor/priest-celebrant. Besides giving participants the opportunity to become familiar with their own part in the wedding ceremony, you may wish to add to the evening preparations by planning its spiritual aspect also.

You may desire to have, after the rehearsal, a short prayer service, a special act of homage to the Blessed Virgin Mary, and/or a penitential celebration of the Word, with the opportunity provided for sacramental confession.

This would be a fitting way to conclude the preparations for the day on which you enter into your special life-long covenant of love with each other.

RITE OF MARRIAGE

INTRODUCTION

RITE FOR CELEBRATING MARRIAGE
DURING MASS

RITE FOR CELEBRATING MARRIAGE
OUTSIDE MASS

RITE FOR CELEBRATING MARRIAGE
BETWEEN A CATHOLIC AND
AN UNBAPTIZED PERSON

TEXTS FOR USE IN THE MARRIAGE RITE
AND IN THE WEDDING MASS:

Scripture Readings
Opening Prayer
Blessing of Rings
Prayers over the Gifts
Prefaces
Nuptial Blessing
Prayers After Communion
Blessing at the End of Mass

present, by which their love is nourished and all are lifted up into communion with our Lord and with one another.[7]

7. Priests should first of all strengthen and nourish the faith of those about to be married, for the sacrament of matrimony presupposes and demands faith.[8]

CHOICE OF RITE

8. *In a marriage between a Catholic and a baptized person who is not Catholic, the regulations which appear on pages 51 to 56 in the right of marriage outside Mass shall be observed.* If suitable, and if the Ordinary of the place gives permission, the rite for celebrating marriage within Mass may be used, except that, according to the general law, communion is not given to the non-Catholic.

In a marriage between a Catholic and one who is not baptized, the rite which appears in nos. 55-66 [pp. 58-62] is to be followed.

9. Furthermore, priests should show special consideration to those who take part in liturgical celebrations or hear the gospel only on the occasion of a wedding, either because they are not Catholics, or because they are Catholics who rarely, if ever, take part in the eucharist or seem to have abandoned the practice of their faith. Priests are ministers of Christ's gospel to everyone.

10. In the celebration of matrimony, apart from the liturgical laws providing for due honors to civil authorities, no special honors are to be paid to any private persons or classes of person, whether in the ceremonies or by external display.[9]

11. Whenever marriage is celebrated during Mass, white vestments are worn and the wedding Mass is used. If the marriage is celebrated on a Sunday or solemnity, the Mass of the day is used with the nuptial blessing and, where appropriate, the special final blessing.

The liturgy of the word is extremely helpful in emphasizing the meaning of the sacrament and the obligations of marriage. When the wedding Mass may not be used, one of the readings on pages 64-89 should be chosen, except from Holy Thursday to Easter and on the feasts of Christmas, Epiphany, Ascension, Pentecost, Corpus Christi, and other holydays of obligation. On the Sundays of the Christmas season and throughout the year, in Masses which are not parish Masses, the wedding Mass may be used without change.

When a marriage is celebrated during Advent or Lent or other days of penance, the parish priest should advise the couple to take into consideration the special nature of these times.

PREPARATION OF LOCAL RITUALS

12. In addition to the faculty spoken of below in no. 17 for regions where the Roman Ritual for matrimony is used, particular rituals shall be prepared, suitable for the customs and needs of individual areas, according to the principle of art. 63b and 77 of the Constitution on the Sacred Liturgy. These are to be reviewed by the Apostolic See.

In making adaptations, the following points must be remembered:

13. The formulas of the Roman Ritual may be adapted or, as the case may be, filled out (including the questions before the consent and the actual words of consent).

When the Roman Ritual has several optional formulas, local rituals may add other formulas of the same type.

14. Within the rite of the sacrament of matrimony, the arrangement of its parts may be varied. If it seems more suitable, even the questions before the consent may be omitted as long as the priest asks and receives the consent of the contracting parties.

15. After the exchange of rings, the crowning or veiling of the bride may take place according to local custom.

In any region where the joining of hands or the blessing or exchange of rings does not fit in with the practice of the people, the conference of bishops may allow these rites to be omitted or other rites substituted.

16. As for the marriage customs of nations that are now receiving the gospel for the first time, whatever is good and is not indissolubly bound up with superstition and error should be sympathetically considered and, if possible, preserved intact. Sometimes the Church admits such things into the liturgy itself, as long as they harmonize with its true and authentic spirit.[10]

RIGHT TO PREPARE A COMPLETELY NEW RITE

17. Each conference of bishops may draw up its own marriage rite suited to the usages of the place and people and approved by the Apostolic See. The rite must always conform to the law that the priest assisting at such marriages must ask for and receive the consent of the contracting parties,[11] and the nuptial blessing should always be given.[12]

18. Among peoples where the marriage ceremonies customarily take place in the home, sometimes over a period of several days, these customs should be adapted to the Christian spirit and to the liturgy. In such cases the conference of bishops, according to the pastoral needs of the people, may allow the sacramental rite to be celebrated in the home.

NOTES

1. Ephesians 5:32.
2. 1 Corinthians 7:7; II Vatican Council, Dogmatic Constitution on the Church, *Lumen Gentium,* 11.
3. II Vatican Council, Constitution on the Church in the Modern World, *Gaudium et Spes,* 48.

4. *Ibid.*, 48, 49.

5. *Ibid.*, 48, 50.

6. II Vatican Council, Constitution on the Sacred Liturgy, *Sacrosanctum Concilium,* 52; S.C.R., Instruction *Inter Oecumenici,* no. 54: AAS 56 (1964) 890.

7. II Vatican Council, Decree on the Apostolate of the Laity, *Apostolicam actuositatem,* 3; Dogmatic Constitution on the Church, *Lumen Gentium,* 12.

8. II Vatican Council, Constitution on the Sacred Liturgy, *Sacrosanctum Concilium,* 59.

9. *Ibid.,* 32.

10. *Ibid.,* 37.

11. *Ibid.,* 77.

12. *Ibid.,* 78.

Rite for Celebrating Marriage During Mass

ENTRANCE RITE

19. At the appointed time, the priest, vested for Mass, goes with the ministers to the door of the church or, if more suitable, to the altar. There he greets the bride and bridegroom in a friendly manner, showing that the Church shares their joy.

Where it is desirable that the rite of welcome be omitted, the celebration of marriage begins at once with the Mass.

20. If there is a procession to the altar, the ministers go first, followed by the priest, and then the bride and bridegroom. According to local custom, they may be escorted by at least their parents and the two witnesses. Meanwhile, the entrance song is sung.

LITURGY OF THE WORD

21. The liturgy of the word is celebrated according to the rubrics. There may be three readings, the first of them from the Old Testament. [See pp. 64-71.]

22. After the gospel, the priest gives a homily drawn from the sacred text. He speaks about the mystery of Christian marriage, the dignity of wedded love, the grace of the sacrament and the responsibilities of married people, keeping in mind the circumstances of this particular marriage.

RITE OF MARRIAGE

23. All stand, including the bride and bridegroom, and the priest addresses them in these or similar words:

My dear friends,° you have come together in this church so that the Lord may seal and strengthen your love in the presence of the Church's minister and this community. Christ abundantly blesses this love. He has already consecrated you in baptism and now he enriches and strengthens you by a special sacrament so that you may assume the duties of marriage in mutual and lasting fidelity. And so, in the presence of the Church, I ask you to state your intentions.

24. The priest then questions them about their freedom of choice, faithfulness to each other, and the acceptance and upbringing of children:

N. and N., have you come here freely and without reservation to give yourselves to each other in marriage?

Will you love and honor each other as man and wife for the rest of your lives?

The following question may be omitted if, for example, the couple is advanced in years.

Will you accept children lovingly from God, and bring them up according to the law of Christ and his Church?

Each answers the questions separately.

CONSENT

25. The priest invites the couple to declare their consent:

Since it is your intention to enter into marriage, join your right hands, and declare your consent before God and his Church.

°At the discretion of the priest, other words which seem more suitable under the circumstances, such as friends, dearly beloved, brethren, may be used. This also applies to parallel instances in the liturgy.

They join hands.
The bridegroom says:

I, N., take you, N., to be my wife. I promise to be true to
you in good times and in bad, in sickness and in health. I
will love you and honor you all the days of my life.

The bride says:

I, N., take you, N., to be my husband. I promise to be
true to you in good times and in bad, in sickness and in
health. I will love you and honor you all the days of my life.

If, however, it seems preferable for pastoral reasons, the priest
may obtain consent from the couple through questions.

First he asks the bridegroom:

N., do you take N. to be your wife? Do you promise to
be true to her in good times and in bad, in sickness and in
health, to love her and honor her all the days of your life?

The bridegroom:

I do.

Then he asks the bride:

N., do you take N. to be your husband? Do you promise
to be true to him in good times and in bad, in sickness and in
health, to love him and honor him all the days of your life?

The bride:

I do.

If pastoral necessity demands it, the conference of bishops may
decree, in virtue of the faculty in no. 17 [p. 36], that the priest
should always obtain the consent of the couple through questions.

In the dioceses of the United States, the following alternative
form may be used:

I, N., take you, N., for my lawful wife (husband), to
have and to hold, from this day forward, for better, for
worse, for richer, for poorer, in sickness and in health, until
death do us part.

If it seems preferable for pastoral reasons for the priest to obtain consent from the couple through questions, in the dioceses of the United States the following alternative form may be used:

N., do you take N. for your lawful wife (husband), to have and to hold, from this day forward, for better, for worse, for richer, for poorer, in sickness and in health, until death do you part?

The bride (bridegroom): I do.

26. Receiving their consent, the priest says:

You have declared your consent before the Church. May the Lord in his goodness strengthen your consent and fill you both with his blessings.

What God has joined, men must not divide.

R. **Amen.**

BLESSING AND EXCHANGE OF RINGS

27. Priest:

(a) May the Lord bless ✛ these rings
which you give to each other
as the sign of your love and fidelity.

R. **Amen.**

Other forms of the blessing of rings:

(b) Lord, bless these rings which we bless ✛ in your name.
Grant that those who wear them
may always have a deep faith in each other.
May they do your will
and always live together
in peace, good will, and love.

(We ask this) through Christ our Lord.

R. **Amen.**

(c) Lord,
bless ✠ and consecrate N. and N.
in their love for each other.
May these rings be a symbol
of true faith in each other,
and always remind them of their love.

Through Christ our Lord.

R. **Amen.**

28. The bridegroom places his wife's ring on her ring finger. He may say:

N., take this ring as a sign of my love and fidelity. In the name of the Father, and of the Son, and of the Holy Spirit.

The bride places her husband's ring on his ring finger. She may say:

N., take this ring as a sign of my love and fidelity. In the name of the Father, and of the Son, and of the Holy Spirit.

29. The general intercessions (prayer of the faithful) follow, using formulas approved by the conference of bishops. If the rubrics call for it, the profession of faith is said after the general intercessions.

LITURGY OF THE EUCHARIST

30. The Order of Mass is followed, with the following changes. During the offertory, the bride and bridegroom may bring the bread and wine to the altar.

31. Proper preface (see nos. 115-117 [pp. 93-95]).

32. When the Roman canon is used, the special Hanc igitur is said (see no. 118 [p. 95]).

NUPTIAL BLESSING

33. After the Lord's Prayer, the prayer *Deliver us* is omitted. The priest faces the bride and bridegroom and, with hands joined, says:

[A] My dear friends, let us turn to the Lord and pray
that he will bless with his grace this woman (or N.)
now married in Christ to this man (or N.)
and that (through the sacrament of the body and blood of
    Christ,)
he will unite in love the couple he has joined in this holy
    bond.

All pray silently for a short while. Then the priest extends his
hands and continues with form A, B, or C:

A Father, by your power you have made everything
    out of nothing.
In the beginning you created the universe
and made mankind in your own likeness.
You gave man the constant help of woman
so that man and woman should no longer be two, but one
    flesh,
and you teach us that what you have united
may never be divided.

B Father, you have made the union of man and wife so
    holy a mystery
that it symbolizes the marriage of Christ and his Church.

C Father, by your plan man and woman are united,
and married life has been established
as the one blessing that was not forfeited by original sin
or washed away in the flood.

The priest continues:

Look with love upon this woman, your daughter,
now joined to her husband in marriage.
She asks your blessing.
Give her the grace of love and peace.
May she always follow the example of the holy women
whose praises are sung in the scriptures.

May her husband put his trust in her
and recognize that she is his equal
and the heir with him to the life of grace.
May he always honor her and love her
as Christ loves his bride, the Church.

Father, keep them always true to your commandments.
Keep them faithful in marriage
and let them be living examples of Christian life.

Give them the strength which comes from the gospel
so that they may be witnesses of Christ to others.
(Bless them with children
and help them to be good parents.
May they live to see their children's children.)
And, after a happy old age,
grant them fullness of life with the saints
in the kingdom of heaven.

(We ask this) through Christ our Lord.

    R. **Amen.**

34. If one or both of the parties will not be receiving communion, the words in the introduction to the nuptial blessing, *through the sacrament of the body and blood of Christ,* may be omitted.

If desired, in the prayer *Father, by your power,* two of the first three paragraphs may be omitted, keeping only the paragraph which corresponds to the reading of the Mass.

In the last paragraph of this prayer, the words in parentheses may be omitted whenever circumstances suggest it, if, for example, the couple is advanced in years.

OTHER FORMS
OF THE NUPTIAL BLESSING:

    B In the following prayer, either the paragraph *Holy Father, you created mankind* or the paragraph *Father, to reveal the plan of your love,* may be omitted, keeping only the paragraph which corresponds to the reading of the Mass.

Let us pray to the Lord for N. and N.
who come to God's altar at the beginning of their married
    life
so that they may always be united in love for each other
(as now they share in the body and blood of Christ).

All pray silently for a short while. Then the priest extends his
hands and continues:

Holy Father, you created mankind in your own image
and made man and woman to be joined as husband and wife
in union of body and heart
and so fulfill their mission in this world.

Father, to reveal the plan of your love,
you made the union of husband and wife
an image of the covenant between you and your people.

In the fulfillment of this sacrament,
the marriage of Christian man and woman
is a sign of the marriage between Christ and the Church.
Father, stretch out your hand, and bless N. and N.

Lord, grant that as they begin to live this sacrament
they may share with each other the gifts of your love
and become one in heart and mind
as witnesses to your presence in their marriage.
Help them to create a home together
(and give them children to be formed by the gospel
and to have a place in your family).

Give your blessings to N., your daughter,
so that she may be a good wife (and mother),
caring for the home,
faithful in love for her husband,
generous and kind.
Give your blessings to N., your son,
so that he may be a faithful husband
(and a good father).

Father, grant that as they come together to your table on earth,
so they may one day have the joy of sharing your feast in heaven.

(We ask this) through Christ our Lord.

R. **Amen.**

 C My dear friends, let us ask God
for his continued blessings upon this bridegroom and his bride (or N. and N.).

All pray silently for a short while. Then the priest extends his hands and continues:

Holy Father, creator of the universe,
maker of man and woman in your own likeness,
source of blessing for married life,
we humbly pray to you for this woman
who today is united with her husband in this sacrament of marriage.

May your fullest blessing come upon her and her husband
so that they may together rejoice in your gift of married love
(and enrich your Church with their children).

Lord, may they both praise you when they are happy
and turn to you in their sorrows.
May they be glad that you help them in their work
and know that you are with them in their need.
May they pray to you in the community of the Church,
and be your witnesses in the world.
May they reach old age in the company of their friends,
and come at last to the kingdom of heaven.

(We ask this) through Christ our Lord.

R. **Amen.**

35. At the words *Let us offer each other the sign of peace,* the married couple and all present show their peace and love for one another in an appropriate way.

36. The married couple may receive communion under both kinds.

BLESSING AT THE END OF MASS

37. Before blessing the people at the end of Mass, the priest blesses the bride and bridegroom, using one of the forms below:

A God the eternal Father keep you in love with each
   other,
so that the peace of Christ may stay with you
and be always in your home.

   R. **Amen.**

May (your children bless you,)
your friends console you
and all men live in peace with you.

   R. **Amen.**

May you always bear witness to the love of God in this
   world
so that the afflicted and the needy
will find in you generous friends,
and welcome you into the joys of heaven.

   R. **Amen.**

And may almighty God bless you all,
the Father, and the Son, ✚ and the Holy Spirit.

   R. **Amen.**

B May God, the almighty Father,
give you his joy
and bless you (in your children).

   R. **Amen.**

May the only Son of God have mercy on you
and help you in good times and in bad.

   R. **Amen.**

May the Holy Spirit of God
always fill your hearts with his love.

   R. **Amen.**

And may almighty God bless you all,
the Father, and the Son, ✟ and the Holy Spirit.

    R. **Amen.**

C May the Lord Jesus, who was a guest at the wedding
    in Cana,
bless you and your families and friends.

    R. **Amen.**

May Jesus, who loved his Church to the end,
always fill your hearts with his love.

    R. **Amen.**

May he grant that, as you believe in his resurrection,
so you may wait for him in joy and hope.

    R. **Amen.**

And may almighty God bless you all,
the Father, and the Son, ✟ and the Holy Spirit.

    R. **Amen.**

D *[In the United States]*
May almighty God, with his Word of blessing, unite your
    hearts in the never-ending bond of pure love.

    R. **Amen.**

May your children bring you happiness, and may your
    generous love for them be returned to you, many times
    over.

    R. **Amen.**

May the peace of Christ live always in your hearts and in
    your home.
May you have true friends to stand by you, both in joy
    and in sorrow.
May you be ready and willing to help and comfort all
    who come to you in need.
And may the blessings promised to the compassionate be
    yours in abundance.

    R. **Amen.**

May you find happiness and satisfaction in your work.

May daily problems never cause you undue anxiety, nor the desire for earthly possessions dominate your lives.

But may your hearts' first desire be always the good things waiting for you in the life of heaven.

R. **Amen.**

May the Lord bless you with many happy years together, so that you may enjoy the rewards of a good life.

And after you have served him loyally in his kingdom on earth, may he welcome you to his eternal kingdom in heaven.

R. **Amen.**

And may almighty God bless you all,
the Father, and the Son, ✠ and the Holy Spirit.

R. **Amen.**

38. If two or more marriages are celebrated at the same time, the questioning before the consent, the consent itself, and the acceptance of consent shall always be done individually for each couple; the rest, including the nuptial blessing, is said once for all, using the plural form.

Rite for Celebrating Marriage Outside Mass[13]

ENTRANCE RITE AND LITURGY OF THE WORD

39. At the appointed time, the priest, wearing surplice and white stole (or a white cope, if desired), proceeds with the ministers to the door of the Church or, if more suitable, to the altar. There he greets the bride and bridegroom in a friendly manner, showing that the Church shares their joy.

Where it is desirable that the rite of welcome be omitted, the celebration of matrimony begins at once with the liturgy of the word.

40. If there is a procession to the altar, the ministers go first, followed by the priest, and then the bride and bridegroom. According to local custom, they may be escorted by at least their parents and the two witnesses. Meanwhile, the entrance song is sung.

Then the people are greeted, and the prayer is offered, unless a brief pastoral exhortation seems more desirable.[14] [See pp. 89-92.]

41. The liturgy of the word takes place in the usual manner. There may be three readings, the first of them from the Old Testament. [See pp. 64-71.]

42. After the gospel, the priest gives a homily drawn from the sacred text. He speaks about the mystery of Christian marriage, the dignity of wedded love, the grace of the sacrament, and the responsibilities of married people, keeping in mind the circumstances of this particular marriage.

RITE OF MARRIAGE

43. All stand, including the bride and bridegroom, and the priest addresses them in these or similar words:

My dear friends, you have come together in this church so that the Lord may seal and strengthen your love in the presence of the Church's minister and this community. Christ abundantly blesses this love. He has already consecrated you in baptism and now he enriches and strengthens you by a special sacrament so that you may assume the duties of marriage in mutual and lasting fidelity. And so, in the presence of the Church, I ask you to state your intentions.

44. The priest then questions them about their freedom of choice, faithfulness to each other, and the acceptance and upbringing of children:

N. and N., have you come here freely and without reservation to give yourselves to each other in marriage?

Will you love and honor each other as man and wife for the rest of your lives?

The following question may be omitted if, for example, the couple is advanced in years.

Will you accept children lovingly from God, and bring them up according to the law of Christ and his Church?

Each answers the questions separately.

CONSENT

45. The priest invites them to declare their consent.

Since it is your intention to enter into marriage, join your right hands, and declare your consent before God and his Church.

They join hands.
The bridegroom says:

I, N., take you, N., to be my wife. I promise to be true to you in good times and in bad, in sickness and in health. I will love you and honor you all the days of my life.

The bride says:

I, N., take you, N., to be my husband. I promise to be true to you in good times and in bad, in sickness and in health. I will love you and honor you all the days of my life.

If, however, it seems preferable for pastoral reasons, the priest may obtain consent from the couple through questions. First he asks the bridegroom:

N., do you take N. to be your wife? Do you promise to be true to her in good times and in bad, in sickness and in health, to love her and honor her all the days of your life?

The bridegroom:

I do.

Then he asks the bride:

N., do you take N. to be your husband? Do you promise to be true to him in good times and in bad, in sickness and in health, to love him and honor him all the days of your life?

The bride:

I do.

If pastoral necessity demands it, the conference of bishops may decree, in virtue of the faculty in no. 17 [p. 36], that the priest should always obtain the consent of the couple through questions.

In the dioceses of the United States, the following form may also be used:

I, N., take you, N., for my lawful wife, to have and to hold, from this day forward, for better, for worse, for richer, for poorer, in sickness and in health, until death do us part.

I, N., take you, N., for my lawful husband, to have and to hold, from this day forward, for better, for worse, for richer, for poorer, in sickness and in health, until death do us part.

If it seems preferable for pastoral reasons for the priest to obtain consent from the couple through questions, in the dioceses of the United States the following alternative form may be used:

N., do you take N. for your lawful wife (husband), to have and to hold, from this day forward, for better, for worse, for richer, for poorer, in sickness and in health, until death do you part?

The bride (bridegroom): I do.

46. Receiving their consent, the priest says:

You have declared your consent before the Church. May the Lord in his goodness strengthen your consent and fill you both with his blessings.

What God has joined, men must not divide.

R. **Amen.**

BLESSING AND EXCHANGE OF RINGS

47. Priest:

May the Lord bless ✚ these rings which you give to each other as the sign of your love and fidelity.

R. **Amen.**

For other forms of the blessing of rings, see nos. 110, 111 [p. 92].

48. The bridegroom places his wife's ring on her ring finger. He may say:

N., take this ring as a sign of my love and fidelity. In the name of the Father, and of the Son, and of the Holy Spirit.

The bride places her husband's ring on his ring finger. She may say:

N., take this ring as a sign of my love and fidelity. In the name of the Father, and of the Son, and of the Holy Spirit.

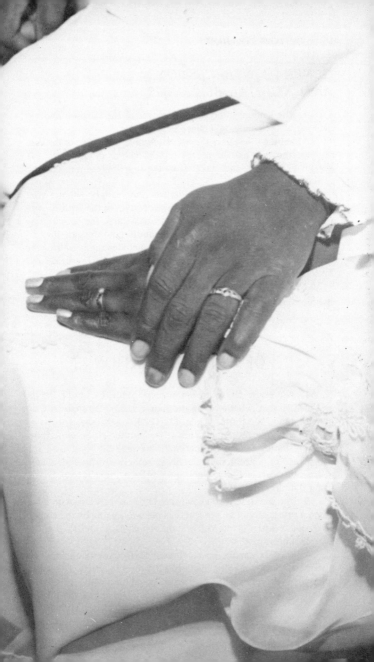

GENERAL INTERCESSIONS
AND NUPTIAL BLESSINGS

49. The general intercessions (prayer of the faithful) and the blessing of the couple take place in this order:

a) First the priest uses the invitatory of any blessing of the couple (see the first part of no. 33 [pp. 42-43], or of nos. 120, 121 [pp. 96, 97]) or any other, taken from the approved formulas for the general intercessions.

b) Immediately after the invitatory, there can be either a brief silence, or a series of petitions from the prayer of the faithful with responses by the people. All the petitions should be in harmony with the blessing which follows, but should not duplicate it.

c) Then, omitting the prayer that concludes the prayer of the faithful, the priest extends his hands and blesses the bride and bridegroom.

50. This blessing may be *Father, by your power,* (no. 33 [p. 43] or another from nos. 120, 121 [pp. 96-98]).

CONCLUSION
OF THE CELEBRATION

51. The entire rite can be concluded with the Lord's Prayer and the blessing, whether with the simple form, *May almighty God,* or with one of the forms in nos. 125-127 [pp. 99-100].

52. If two or more marriages are celebrated at the same time, the questioning before the consent, the consent itself, and the acceptance of consent shall always be done individually for each couple; the rest, including the nuptial blessing, is said once for all, using the plural form.

53. The rite described above should be used by a deacon who, when a priest cannot be present, has been delegated by the bishop or pastor to assist at the celebration of marriage, and to give the Church's blessing.[15]

54. If Mass cannot be celebrated and communion is to be distributed during the rite, the Lord's Prayer is said first. After communion, a reverent silence may be observed for a while, or a psalm or song of praise may be sung or recited. Then comes the prayer,

Lord, we who have shared (no. 123 [p. 98], if only the bride and bridegroom receive), or the prayer, *God, who in this wondrous sacrament* or other suitable prayer.

The rite ends with a blessing, either the simple formula, *May almighty God bless you,* or one of the forms in nos. 125-127 [pp. 99-100].

NOTES

13. According to the words of the Constitution on the Sacred Liturgy, *Sacrosanctum concilium,* repeated in no. 6 of the introduction above, the celebration of marriage normally takes place during Mass. Nevertheless, a good reason can excuse from the celebration of Mass (Sacred Congregation of Rites, Instruction, *Inter Oecumenici,* no. 70: AAS 56 [1964] 893), and sometimes even urges that Mass should be omitted. In this case the rite for celebrating marriage outside Mass should be used.

14. II Vatican Council, Sacred Congregation of Rites, Instruction, *Inter Oecumenici,* no. 74: AAS 56 (1964) 894.

15. Paul VI, motu proprio, *Sacram Diaconatus Ordinem,* June 18, 1967, no. 22, 4: AAS 59 (1967) 702.

Rite for Celebrating Marriage Between a Catholic and an Unbaptized Person

If marriage is celebrated between a Catholic and an unbaptized person (either a catechumen or a non-Christian), the rite may be performed in the church or some other suitable place and takes the following form.

RITE OF WELCOME AND LITURGY OF THE WORD

55. At the appointed time, the priest wearing surplice and white stole (or a white cope if desired), proceeds with the ministers to the door of the church or to another appropriate place and greets the bride and the bridegroom.

Where it is desirable that the rite of welcome be omitted, the celebration of marriage begins at once with the liturgy of the word.

56. The liturgy of the word takes place in the usual manner. There may be three readings, the first of them from the Old Testament. If circumstances make it more desirable, there may be a single reading. [See pp. 64-71.]

57. A homily, drawn from the sacred text, is given and should speak of the obligations of marriage and other appropriate points.

RITE OF MARRIAGE

58. All stand, including the bride and the bridegroom. The priest addresses them in these or similar words:

My dear friends, you have come togèther in this church so that the Lord may seal and strengthen your love in the presence of the Church's minister and this community. In this way you will be strengthened to keep mutual and lasting faith with each other and to carry out the other duties of marriage. And so, in the presence of the Church, I ask you to state your intentions.

59. The priest then questions them about their freedom of choice, faithfulness to each other, and the acceptance and upbringing of children.

N. and N., have you come here freely and without reservation to give yourselves to each other in marriage?

Will you love and honor each other as man and wife for the rest of your lives?

The following question may be omitted if, for example, the couple is advanced in years.

Will you accept children lovingly from God, and bring them up according to the law of Christ and his Church?

Each answers the questions separately.

CONSENT

60. The priest invites them to declare their consent. °

Since it is your intention to enter into marriage, join your right hands, and declare your consent before God and his Church.

They join hands.
The bridegroom says:

I, N., take you, N., to be my wife. I promise to be true to you in good times and in bad, in sickness and in health. I will love you and honor you all the days of my life.

°In the dioceses of the United States, an alternative form may be used as given on pp. 39-41.

The bride says:

I, N., take you, N., to be my husband. I promise to be true to you in good times and in bad, in sickness and in health. I will love you and honor you all the days of my life.

If, however, it seems preferable for pastoral reasons, the priest may obtain consent from the couple through questions. First he asks the bridegroom:

N., do you take N. to be your wife? Do you promise to be true to her in good times and in bad, in sickness and in health, to love her and honor her all the days of your life?

The bridegroom:

I do.

Then he asks the bride:

N., do you take N. to be your husband? Do you promise to be true to him in good times and in bad, in sickness and in health, to love him and honor him all the days of your life?

The bride:

I do.

If pastoral necessity demands it, the conference of bishops may decree in virtue of the faculty in no. 17 [p. 36], that the priest should always obtain the consent of the couple through questions.

61. Receiving their consent, the priest says:

You have declared your consent before the Church. May the Lord in his goodness strengthen your consent and fill you both with his blessings.

What God has joined, men must not divide.

R. **Amen.**

BLESSING AND EXCHANGE OF RINGS

62. If circumstances so require, the blessing and exchange of rings can be omitted. If this rite is observed, the priest says:

May the Lord bless ✠ these rings which you give to each other as the sign of your love and fidelity.

R. **Amen.**

For other forms of the blessing of rings, see nos. 110, 111 [p. 92].

63. The bridegroom places his wife's ring on her ring finger. He may say:

N., take this ring as a sign of my love and fidelity.
In the name of the Father, and of the Son, and of the Holy Spirit.

The bride places her husband's ring on his ring finger. She may say:

N. take this ring as a sign of my love and fidelity.
In the name of the Father, and of the Son, and of the Holy Spirit.

GENERAL INTERCESSIONS AND NUPTIAL BLESSINGS

64. If circumstances so require, the blessing of the bride and bridegroom can be omitted. If used, it is combined with the general intercessions (prayer of the faithful) in this order:

a) First the priest uses the invitatory of any blessing of the couple (see the first part of no. 33 [pp. 42-43], or of nos. 120, 121 [pp. 96, 97]) or any other, taken from any approved formula for the general intercessions.

b) Immediately after the invitatory, there can be either a brief period of silence, or a series of petitions from the prayer of the faithful with responses by the people. All the petitions should be in harmony with the blessing which follows, but should not duplicate it.

c) Then, omitting the prayer that concludes the prayer of the faithful, the priest blesses the bride and bridegroom:

65. Facing them, he joins his hands and says:

My brothers and sisters, let us ask God
for his continued blessings upon this bridegroom and his bride.

All pray silently for a short while. Then the priest extends his hands and continues:

Holy Father, creator of the universe,
maker of man and woman in your own likeness,

source of blessing for the married life,
we humbly pray to you for this bride
who today is united with her husband in the bond of marriage.

May your fullest blessing come upon her and her husband
so that they may together rejoice in your gift of married
   love.
May they be noted for their good lives,
(and be parents filled with virtue).

Lord, may they both praise you when they are happy
and turn to you in their sorrows.
May they be glad that you help them in their work,
and know that you are with them in their need.
May they reach old age in the company of their friends,
and come at last to the kingdom of heaven.

(We ask this) through Christ our Lord.
   R. **Amen.**

CONCLUSION
OF THE CELEBRATION

66. The rite may be concluded with the Lord's Prayer (or, if the
nuptial blessing has been omitted, another prayer by the priest) and
a blessing using the customary form, *May almighty God bless you* or
another formula from nos. 125-127 [pp. 99-100].

Texts for Use in the Marriage Rite and in the Wedding Mass

SCRIPTURE READINGS

The following Scripture passages have been taken from translations approved for use in the Liturgy:

The New American Bible (indicated by one asterisk: *)

The Jerusalem Bible (indicated by two asterisks: **)

Revised Standard Version (Catholic Edition).

Should you prefer one particular translation, you may certainly consult with your pastor in this regard.

The pastoral reflections that precede the Scripture texts are based on the chapter, "The Dignity of Marriage and Family Life," from Vatican II's document *Gaudium et spes:* "Pastoral Constitution on the Church in the Modern World," nos. 47-52.

OLD TESTAMENT READING

1 From the book of Genesis 1:26-28, 31   [67]

God Himself is the Author of matrimony, endowed as it is with various benefits and purposes. Love and marriage tend by nature itself to the procreation and educa-

tion of children, the supreme gift of married love. Let married couples then be collaborators in their God-given roles of transmitting human life and make this their own proper mission in life.

"God said, 'Let us make man in our image, after our likeness; and let them have dominion over the fish of the sea, and over the birds of the air, and over the cattle, and over all the earth, and over every creeping thing that creeps upon the earth.' So God created man in his own image, in the image of God he created him; male and female he created them. And God blessed them, and God said to them, 'Be fruitful and multiply, and fill the earth and subdue it; and have dominion over the fish of the sea and over the birds of the air and over every living thing that moves upon the earth.' And God saw everything that he had made, and behold, it was very good."

2   From the book of Genesis 2:18-24   [68]

The intimate partnership of married life and love has been established by the Creator and qualified by His laws, and is rooted in the conjugal covenant of irrevocable personal consent. Hence by that human act whereby spouses mutually bestow and accept each other a relationship arises which by divine will and in the eyes of society too is a lasting one.

"Then the Lord God said, 'It is not good that the man should be alone; I will make him a helper fit for him.' So out of the ground the Lord God formed every beast of the field and every bird of the air, and brought them to the man to see what he would call them; and whatever the man called every living creature, that was its name. The man gave names to all cattle, and to the birds of the air, and to every beast of the field; but for the man there was not found a helper fit for him. So the Lord God caused a deep sleep to fall upon the man, and while he slept took one of his ribs and closed up its place with flesh; and the rib which the

Lord God had taken from the man he made into a woman and brought her to the man. Then the man said,

'This at last is bone of my bones
    and flesh of my flesh;
she shall be called Woman,
    because she was taken out of Man.'

"Therefore a man leaves his father and his mother and cleaves to his wife, and they become one flesh."

3   From the book of Genesis 24:48-51, 58-67   [69]

In expressing their free consent the spouses take a marriage vow that accords with the God-given nature of this sacred bond. This point is really central, for on the stability of married life of man and woman depends the continuation of the race, the personal growth and final destiny of family members, and the dignity and peace of the whole family of man.

The servant of Abraham said to Laban: "Then I bowed my head and worshiped the Lord, and blessed the Lord, the God of my master Abraham, who had led me by the right way to take the daughter of my master's kinsman for his son. Now then, if you will deal loyally and truly with my master, tell me; and if not, tell me; that I may turn to the right hand or to the left."

Then Laban and Bethuel answered, "The thing comes from the Lord; we cannot speak to you bad or good. Behold, Rebekah is before you, take her and go, and let her be the wife of your master's son, as the Lord has spoken."

And they called Rebekah, and said to her, "Will you go with this man?" She said, "I will go." So they sent away Rebekah their sister and her nurse, and Abraham's servant and his men. And they blessed Rebekah, and said to her, "Our sister, be the mother of thousands of ten thousands; and may your descendants possess the gate of those who hate them!" Then Rebekah and her maids arose, and rode upon the camels and followed the man; thus the servant took Rebekah, and went his way.

Now Isaac had come from Beerlahairoi, and was dwelling in the Negeb. And Isaac went out to meditate in the field in the evening; and he lifted up his eyes and looked, and behold, there were camels coming. And Rebekah lifted up her eyes, and when she saw Isaac, she alighted from the camel, and said to the servant, "Who is the man yonder, walking in the field to meet us?" The servant said, "It is my master." So she took her veil and covered herself. And the servant told Isaac all the things that he had done. Then Isaac brought her into the tent, and took Rebekah, and she became his wife; and he loved her. So Isaac was comforted after his mother's death.

4   From the book of Tobit 7:9-10, 11-15*   [70]

A healthy marriage and a happy family life lie at the foundations not only of sound personal growth but of the whole structure of society as well.

Tobiah said to Raphael, "Brother Azariah, ask Raguel to let me marry my kinswoman Sarah." Raguel overheard the words; so he said to the boy: "Eat and drink and be merry tonight, for no man is more entitled to marry my daughter Sarah than you, brother. Besides, not even I have the right to give her to anyone but you, because you are my closest relative. But I will explain the situation to you very frankly. She is yours according to the decree of the Book of Moses. Your marriage to her has been decided in heaven! Take your kinswoman; from now on you are her love, and she is your beloved. She is yours today and ever after. And tonight, son, may the Lord of heaven prosper you both. May he grant you mercy and peace." Then Raguel called his daughter Sarah, and she came to him. He took her by the hand and gave her to Tobiah with the words: "Take her according to the law. According to the decree written in the Book of Moses she is your wife. Take her and bring her back safely to your father.

And may the God of heaven grant both of you peace and prosperity.'' He then called her mother and told her to bring a scroll, so that he might draw up a marriage contract stating that he gave Sarah to Tobiah as his wife according to the decree of the Mosaic law. Her mother brought the scroll, and he drew up the contract, to which they affixed their seals.

Afterward they began to eat and drink.

5 From the book of Tobit 8:5-7 *   [71]

Caught up in the mystery of God's love, the spouses are brought ever closer to Him and are strengthened for their duties as parents. They grow in the spirit of Christ and in the spirit of faith, hope, and charity for the glory of their Creator.

On their wedding night Sarah got up, and she and Tobiah started to pray and beg that deliverance might be theirs. He began with these words:
''Blessed are you, O God of our fathers;
   praised be your name forever and ever.
Let the heavens and all your creation
   praise you forever.
You made Adam and you gave him his wife Eve
   to be his help and support;
   and from these two the human race descended.
You said, 'It is not good for the man to be alone;
   let us make him a partner like himself.'
Now, Lord, you know that I take this wife of mine
   not because of lust,
   but for a noble purpose.
Call down your mercy on me and on her,
   and allow us to live together to a happy old age.''

6 From the Song of Songs 2:8-10, 14, 16; 8:6-7   [72]

The biblical Word of God several times urges the betrothed and the married to nourish and develop their wedlock by pure conjugal love and undivided affection.

This love is an eminently human one since it is directed from one person to another through an affection of the will; it involves the good of the whole person, and therefore can enrich the expressions of body and mind with a unique dignity, ennobling these expressions as special ingredients and signs of the friendship distinctive of marriage.

The voice of my beloved!
   Behold, he comes,
leaping upon the mountains,
   bounding over the hills.
My beloved is like a gazelle,
   or a young stag.
Behold, there he stands
   behind our wall,
gazing in at the windows,
   looking through the lattice.
My beloved speaks and says to me:
"Arise, my love, my fair one,
   and come away.
O my dove, in the clefts of the rock,
   in the covert of the cliff,
let me see your face,
   let me hear your voice,
for your voice is sweet,
   and your face is comely.

My beloved is mine and I am his.
   [He said to me:]
Set me as a seal upon your heart,
   as a seal upon your arm;
for love is strong as death,
   jealousy is cruel as the grave.
Its flashes are flashes of fire,
   a most vehement flame.
Many waters cannot quench love,
   neither can floods drown it."

7   From the book of Sirach 26:1-4, 13-16   [73]

In both Scripture and secular literature the love between husband and wife is highly exalted; and rightly so, for as a deeply human experience, married love so refines the natural affection between two human persons that each seeks the good of the other and in spiritual friendship cherishes the other as another self. Two individuals become "we."

Happy is the husband of a good wife;
   the number of his days will be doubled.
A loyal wife rejoices her husband,
   and he will complete his years in peace.
A good wife is a great blessing;
   she will be granted among the blessings of the man who
      fears the Lord.
Whether rich or poor, his heart is glad,
   and at all times his face is cheerful.

A wife's charm delights her husband,
   and her skill puts fat on his bones.
A silent wife is a gift of the Lord,
   and there is nothing so precious as a disciplined soul.
A modest wife adds charm to charm,
   and no balance can weigh the value of a chaste soul.
Like the sun rising in the heights of the Lord,
   so is the beauty of a good wife in her well-ordered home.

8   From the book of the prophet Jeremiah   [74]
31:31-32, 33-34

The intimate partnership of life and love, which is marriage, deserves the name "covenant," because it comes about by the mutual promise of a freely consenting man and woman and by the will of the Creator is meant to last for a lifetime.

"Behold the days are coming, says the Lord, when I will make a new covenant with the house of Israel and the house of Judah, not like the covenant which I made with their fathers when I took them by the hand to bring them out of the land of Egypt. But this is the covenant which I will make with the house of Israel after those days, says the Lord: I will put my law within them, and I will write it upon their hearts; and I will be their God, and they shall be my people. And no longer shall each man teach his neighbor and each his brother, saying, 'Know the Lord,' for they shall all know me, from the least of them to the greatest, says the Lord.''

NEW TESTAMENT READING

1   From the letter of Paul to the Romans   [75]
8:31-35, 37-39**

Sealed by mutual faithfulness and hallowed above all by Christ's sacrament, this love remains steadfastly true in body and in mind, in bright days or dark.

With God on our side who can be against us? Since God did not spare his own Son, but gave him up to benefit us all, we may be certain, after such a gift, that he will not refuse anything he can give. Could anyone accuse those that God has chosen? When God acquits, could anyone condemn? Could Christ Jesus? No! He not only died for us—he rose from the dead, and there at God's right hand he stands and pleads for us.

Nothing therefore can come between us and the love of Christ, even if we are troubled or worried, or being persecuted, or lacking food or clothes, or being threatened or even attacked. These are the trials through which we triumph, by the power of him who loved us.

For I am certain of this: neither death nor life, no angel, no prince, nothing that exists, nothing still to come, not any power, or height or depth, nor any created thing, can ever come between us and the love of God made visible in Christ Jesus our Lord.

2   From the letter of Paul to the Romans   [76]
12:1-2, 9-18 or 12:1-2, 9-13**

The constant fulfillment of the duties of this Christian vocation demands notable virtue. For this reason, strengthened by grace for holiness of life, the couple will painstakingly cultivate and pray for steadiness of love, largeheartedness and the spirit of sacrifice.

Long form follows; for short form omit what is in brackets.

Think of God's mercy, my brothers, and worship him, I beg you, in a way that is worthy of thinking beings, by offering your living bodies as a holy sacrifice, truly pleasing to God. Do not model yourselves on the behavior of the world around you, but let your behavior change, modeled by your new mind. This is the only way to discover the will of God and know what is good, what it is that God wants, what is the perfect thing to do.

Do not let your love be a pretense, but sincerely prefer good to evil. Love each other as much as brothers should, and have a profound respect for each other. Work for the Lord with untiring effort and with great earnestness of spirit. If you have hope, this will make you cheerful. Do not give up if trials come; and keep on praying. If any of the saints are in need you must share with them; and you should make hospitality your special care.

[Bless those who persecute you: never curse them, bless them. Rejoice with those who rejoice and be sad with those in sorrow. Treat everyone with equal kindness; never be condescending but make real friends with the poor. Do not allow yourself to become self-satisfied. Never repay evil with evil but let everyone see that you are interested only in the highest ideals. Do all you can to live at peace with everyone.]

3   **From the first letter of Paul to the**   [77]
      Corinthians 6:13-15, 17-20**

*Let married people, conscious that they are created in
the image of God and enjoy the dignity of children of God,
strive within their exalted vocation to become witnesses of
that love which Christ revealed to the world.*

The body—this is not meant for fornication; it is for the
Lord, and the Lord for the body. God, who raised the Lord
from the dead, will by his power raise us up too.

You know, surely, that your bodies are members making up the body of Christ. But anyone who is joined to the
Lord is one spirit with him.

Keep away from fornication. All the other sins are com-
mitted outside the body; but to fornicate is to sin against
your own body. Your body, you know, is the temple of the
Holy Spirit, who is in you since you received him from God.
You are not your own property; you have been bought and
paid for. That is why you should use your body for the glory
of God.

4   **From the first letter of Paul to the**   [78]
      Corinthians 12:31—13:8**

*Like Christ's love the love of the spouses is growing
and creative, and like Christ's love expresses itself in giving, in sharing, in serving.*

Be ambitious for the higher gifts. And I am going to
show you a way that is better than any of them.

If I have all the eloquence of men or of angels, but speak
without love, I am simply a gong booming or a cymbal
clashing. If I have the gift of prophecy, understanding all the
mysteries there are, and knowing everything, and if I have
faith in all its fullness, to move mountains, but without love,
then I am nothing at all. If I give away all that I possess,
piece by piece, and if I even let them take my body to burn
it, but am without love, it will do me no good whatever.

Love is always patient and kind; it is never jealous; love is never boastful or conceited; it is never rude or selfish; it does not take offense, and is not resentful. Love takes no pleasure in other people's sins but delights in the truth; it is always ready to excuse, to trust, to hope, and to endure whatever comes.

Love does not come to an end.

5   From the letter of Paul to the Ephesians   [79]
   5:2, 21-33 or 5:2, 25-32**

Like the covenant of old between God and His people, Christ the Lord, as the divine Lover of the Church, unites Christian couples through the sacred covenant of Matrimony, a sacrament and sign of Christ's love of His Church.

Long form follows; for short form omit what is in brackets.

Try, then, to imitate God, as children of his that he loves, and follow Christ by loving as he loved you, giving himself up in our place.

[Give way to one another in obedience to Christ. Wives should regard their husbands as they regard the Lord, since as Christ is the head of the Church and saves the whole body, so is a husband the head of his wife; and as the Church submits to Christ, so should wives to their husbands, in everything.] Husbands should love their wives just as Christ loved the Church and sacrificed himself for her to make her holy. He made her clean by washing her in water with a form of words, so that when he took her to himself she would be glorious, with no speck or wrinkle or anything like that, but holy and faultless. In the same way, husbands must love their wives as they love their own bodies; for a man to love his wife is for him to love himself. A man never hates his own body, but he feeds it and looks after it; and that is the way Christ treats the Church, because it is his body—and we are its living parts. *For this reason, a man must leave his father and mother and be joined to his wife, and the two will become one body.* This mystery has many implications; but I am saying it applies to Christ and the Church. [To sum up; you too, each one of you, must love his wife as he loves himself; and let every wife respect her husband.]

6   From the letter of Paul to the Colossians   [80]
3:12-17**

Growth in holiness involves the whole family, for children reflect the lives of faithful love of their father and mother who are the first heralds of the faith.

You are God's chosen race, his saints; he loves you, and you should be clothed in sincere compassion, in kindness and humility, gentleness and patience. Bear with one another; forgive each other as soon as a quarrel begins. The Lord has forgiven you; now you must do the same. Over all these clothes, to keep them together and complete them, put on love. And may the peace of Christ reign in your hearts, because it is for this that you were called together as parts of one body. Always be thankful.

Let the message of Christ, in all its richness, find a home with you. Teach each other, and advise each other, in all wisdom. With gratitude in your hearts sing psalms and hymns and inspired songs to God; and never say or do anything except in the name of the Lord Jesus, giving thanks to God the Father through him.

7   From the first letter of Peter 3:1-9**   [81]

As a school for human enrichment, family life must be characterized by harmony of minds and hearts especially in all that concerns the education of children. The father's active presence is as vital as is the loving care of the mother within the home.

Wives should be obedient to their husbands. Then, if there are some husbands who have not yet obeyed the word, they may find themselves won over, without a word spoken, by the way their wives behave, when they see how faithful and conscientious they are. Do not dress up for show: doing up your hair, wearing gold bracelets and fine clothes; all this should be inside, in a person's heart, imperishable: the ornament of a sweet and gentle disposition—this is what is precious in the sight of God. That was how the holy women of the past dressed themselves attractively —they hoped in God and were tender and obedient to their husbands; like Sarah, who was obedient to Abraham, and called him her *lord*. You are now her children, as long as you live good lives and do not give way to fear or worry.

In the same way, husbands must always treat their wives with consideration in their life together, respecting a woman as one who, though she may be the weaker partner, is equally an heir to the life of grace. This will stop anything from coming in the way of your prayers.

Finally: you should all agree among yourselves and be sympathetic; love the brothers, have compassion and be self-effacing. Never pay back one wrong with another, or an angry word with another one; instead, pay back with a blessing. That is what you are called to do, so that you inherit a blessing yourself.

8   From the first letter of John 3:18-24 * *   [82]

With a truly human and Christian sense of responsibility, let couples form their judgments regarding the begetting of children in accord with God's own law. Although they do make their own decisions in this matter, they are to be docile and submissive to the Church's teaching office, which authentically interprets God's law in the light of the Gospel. This divine law reveals and enlightens the full meaning of married love and leads it to a truly human wholeness.

My children,
our love is not to be just words or mere talk,
but something real and active;
only by this can we be certain

that we are children of the truth
and be able to quieten our conscience in his presence,
whatever accusations it may raise against us,
because God is greater than our conscience and he
    knows everything.
My dear people,
if we cannot be condemned by our own conscience,
we need not be afraid in God's presence,
and whatever we ask him,
we shall receive,
because we keep his commandments
and live the kind of life that he wants.
His commandments are these:
that we believe in the name of his Son Jesus Christ
and that we love one another
as he told us to.
Whoever keeps his commandments
lives in God and God lives in him.
We know that he lives in us
by the Spirit that he has given us.

9 From the first letter of John 4:7-12 * *   [83]

*Authentic married love is caught up into divine love.
This love God has judged worthy of special gifts, healing,
perfecting and exalting gifts of grace and of charity.*

My dear people,
let us love one another
since love comes from God
and everyone who loves is begotten by God and knows God.
Anyone who fails to love can never have known God,
because God is love.
God's love for us was revealed
when God sent into the world his only Son
so that we could have life through him;
this is the love I mean:
not our love for God, but God's love for us when he sent his
    Son

to be the sacrifice that takes our sins away.
My dear people,
since God has loved us so much,
we too should love one another.
No one has ever seen God;
but as long as we love one another
God will live in us
and his love will be complete in us.

10   From the book of Revelation 19:1, 5-9** [84]

The Christian family, which springs from marriage as a reflection of the loving covenant uniting Christ with the Church, and as a participation in that covenant, will manifest to all men Christ's living presence in the world and the genuine nature of the Church.

After this I seemed to hear the great sound of a huge crowd in heaven, singing, "Alleluia! Victory and glory and power to our God!"

Then a voice came from the throne; it said, "Praise our God, you servants of his and *all who, great or small, revere him.*" And I seemed to hear the voices of a huge crowd, like the sound of the ocean or the great roar of thunder, answering, "Alleluia! The reign of the Lord our God Almighty has begun; let us be glad and joyful and give praise to God, because this is the time for the marriage of the Lamb. His bride is ready, and she has been able to dress herself in dazzling white linen, because her linen is made of the good deeds of the saints." The angel said, "Write this: Happy are those who are invited to the wedding feast of the Lamb."

RESPONSORIAL PSALM

1   Psalm 33:12, 18, 20-21, 22* [85]

R. The earth is full of the goodness of the Lord.
Happy the nation whose God is the Lord,
　　the people he has chosen for his own inheritance.

But see, the eyes of the Lord are upon those who fear him,
  upon those who hope for his kindness. **Repeat response.**
Our soul waits for the Lord,
  who is our help and our shield,
For in him our hearts rejoice;
  in his holy name we trust. **Response.**
May your kindness, O Lord, be upon us
  who have put our hope in you. **Response.**

2   Psalm 34:2-3, 4-5, 6-7, 8-9*   [86]

R. I will bless the Lord at all times.
Or: **R. Taste and see the goodness of the Lord.**
I will bless the Lord at all times;
  his praise shall be ever in my mouth.
Let my soul glory in the Lord;
  the lowly will hear me and be glad. **Repeat response.**
Glorify the Lord with me,
  let us together extol his name
I sought the Lord, and he answered me
  and delivered me from all my fears. **Response.**
Look to him that you may be radiant with joy,
  and your faces may not blush with shame.
When the afflicted man called out, the Lord heard,
  and from all his distress he saved him. **Response.**
The angel of the Lord encamps
  around those who fear him, and delivers them.
Taste and see how good the Lord is;
  happy the man who takes refuge in him. **Response.**

3   Psalm 103:1-2, 8, 13, 17-18*   [87]

R. The Lord is kind and merciful.
Or: **R. The Lord's kindness is everlasting to those
  who fear him.**
Bless the Lord, O my soul;
  and all my being, bless his holy name.

Bless the Lord, O my soul,
  and forget not all his benefits. **Repeat response.**
Merciful and gracious is the Lord,
  slow to anger and abounding in kindness.
As a father has compassion on his children,
  so the Lord has compassion on those who fear him.
    Response.
But the kindness of the Lord is from eternity
  to eternity toward those who fear him,
And his justice toward children's children
  among those who keep his covenant. **Response.**

4 **Psalm 112:1-2, 3-4, 5-7, 7-8, 9***   [88]

  R. Happy are those who do what the Lord commands.
  Or: **R. Alleluia.**

Happy the man who fears the Lord,
  who greatly delights in his commands.
His posterity shall be mighty upon the earth;
  the upright generation shall be blessed. **Repeat response.**
Wealth and riches shall be in his house;
  his generosity shall endure forever.
He dawns through the darkness, a light for the upright;
  he is gracious and merciful and just. **Response.**
Well for the man who is gracious and lends,
  who conducts his affairs with justice;
He shall never be moved;
  the just man shall be in everlasting remembrance.
    Response.
An evil report he shall not fear;
  his heart is firm, trusting in the Lord.
His heart is steadfast; he shall not fear
  Till he looks down upon his foes. **Response.**
Lavishly he gives to the poor;
  his generosity shall endure forever;
  his horn shall be exalted in glory. **Response.**

5   Psalm 128:1-2, 3, 4-5*   [89]

R. Happy are those who fear the Lord.
Or: **R. See how the Lord blesses those who fear him.**
Happy are you who fear the Lord,
  who walk in his ways!
For you shall eat the fruit of your handiwork;
  happy shall you be, and favored. **Repeat response.**
Your wife shall be like a fruitful vine
  in the recesses of your home;
Your children like olive plants
  around your table. **Response.**
Behold, thus is the man blessed
  who fears the Lord.
The Lord bless you from Zion:
  may you see the prosperity of Jerusalem
  all the days of your life. **Response.**

6   Psalm 145:8-9, 10, 15. 17-18*   [90]

R. The Lord is compassionate to all his creatures.
The Lord is gracious and merciful,
  slow to anger and of great kindness.
The Lord is good to all
  and compassionate toward all his works. **Repeat
    response.**
Let all your works give you thanks, O Lord,
  and let your faithful ones bless you.
The eyes of all look hopefully to you,
  and you give them their food in due season. **Response.**
The Lord is just in all his ways
  and holy in all his works.
The Lord is near to all who call upon him,
  to all who call upon him in truth. **Response.**

7   Psalm 148:1-2, 3-4, 9-10, 11-12, 12-14*   [91]

R. Let all praise the name of the Lord.
Or: **R. Alleluia.**

Praise the Lord from the heavens,
  praise him in the heights;
Praise him, all you his angels,
  praise him, all you his hosts. **Repeat response.**
Praise him, sun and moon;
  praise him, all you shining stars.
Praise him, you highest heavens,
  and you waters above the heavens. **Response.**
You mountains and all you hills,
  you fruit trees and all you cedars;
You wild beasts and all tame animals,
  you creeping things and you winged fowl. **Response.**
Let the kings of the earth and all peoples,
  the princes and all the judges of the earth,
Young men too, and maidens,
  old men and boys. **Response.**
Praise the name of the Lord,
  for his name alone is exalted;
His majesty is above earth and heaven,
  and he has lifted up the horn of his people. **Response.**

ALLELUIA VERSE
AND VERSE BEFORE THE GOSPEL

1 1 Jn. 4:8, 11*   [92]

  God is love;
  let us love one another as he has loved us.

2 1 Jn. 4:12*   [93]

  If we love one another,
  God will live in us in perfect love.

3 1 Jn. 4:16*   [94]

  He who lives in love, lives in God,
  and God in him.

4   1 Jn. 4:7*   [95]

Everyone who loves is born of God and knows him.

GOSPEL

1   From the holy gospel according to Matthew   [96]
  5:1-12*

By virtue of the sacrament of Matrimony, as spouses fulfill their conjugal and family obligation, they are penetrated with the spirit of Christ, which suffuses their whole lives with faith, hope and charity. Thus they increasingly advance the perfection of their own personalities, as well as their mutual sanctification, and hence contribute jointly to the glory of God.

When Jesus saw the crowds he went up on the mountainside. After he had sat down his disciples gathered around him, and he began to teach them:

"How blest are the poor in spirit: the reign of God is
  theirs.

Blest too are the sorrowing; they shall be consoled.

[Blest are the lowly; they shall inherit the land.]

Blest are they who hunger and thirst for holiness; they shall have their fill.

Blest are they who show mercy; mercy shall be theirs.

Blest are the single-hearted for they shall see God.

Blest too the peacemakers; they shall be called sons of
  God.

Blest are those persecuted for holiness' sake; the reign of
  God is theirs.

Blest are you when they insult you and persecute you
  and utter every kind of slander against you because
  of me.

Be glad and rejoice, for your reward is great in heaven."

2   From the holy gospel according to Matthew   [97]
5:13-16*

*As a glowing lamp, their way of life of perfect har-
mony, of fidelity to each other, and of devoted concern for
the upbringing of their children will shine out as a witness
to the total renewal of marriage and family life.*

Jesus said to his disciples: "You are the salt of the earth.
But what if salt goes flat? How can you restore its flavor?
Then it is good for nothing but to be thrown out and
trampled underfoot.

"You are the light of the world. A city set on a hill cannot be hidden. Men do not light a lamp and then put it under
a bushel basket. They set it on a stand where it gives light to
all in the house. In the same way, your light must shine
before men so that they may see goodness in your acts and
give praise to your heavenly Father."

3   From the holy gospel according to Matthew   [98]
7:21, 24-29 or 7:21, 24-25*

*The human family, firmly rooted in God, will manifest
to all men the divine Savior's living presence in the world
and the real beauty of the Church which is His spouse.*

Long form follows; for short form omit what is in brackets.

Jesus said to his disciples: "None of those who cry out,
'Lord, Lord,' will enter the kingdom of God but only the one
who does the will of my Father in heaven.

"Anyone who hears my words and puts them into practice is like the wise man who built his house on rock. When
the rainy season set in, the torrents came and the winds
blew, and buffeted his house. It did not collapse; it had been
solidly set on rock. [Anyone who hears my words but does
not put them into practice is like the foolish man who built
his house on sandy ground. The rains fell, the torrents came,
the winds blew and lashed against his house. It collapsed
under all this and was completely ruined."

Jesus finished this discourse and left the crowds spell-bound at his teaching. The reason was that he taught with authority and not like the scribes.]

4   From the holy gospel according to Matthew   [99]
19:3-6*

Through the acts proper to marriage, which are noble and honorable, spouses grow in love: a chaste union enriching both in joy and gratitude. This vital unity of heart and mind and will, excluding adultery, divorce, and every inequality of the sexes, demands the greatest courage, the courage of faithful, truly generous hearts. Let spouses find in God, who is ever faithful, the source of their strength.

Some Pharisees came up to Jesus and said, to test him, "May a man divorce his wife for any reason whatever?" He replied, "Have you not read that at the beginning the Creator made them male and female and declared, 'For this reason a man shall leave his father and mother and cling to his wife, and the two shall become as one'? Thus they are no longer two but one flesh. Therefore, let no man separate what God has joined."

5   From the holy gospel according to Matthew   [100]
22:35-40*

Married love, merging the human with the divine, leads the spouses to a free and mutual gift of themselves, a gift proving itself by gentle affection and by deed; such love pervades the whole of their lives: Indeed by its busy generosity it grows better and grows greater.

One of the Pharisees, a lawyer, in an attempt to trip Jesus up, asked him, "Teacher, which commandment of the law is the greatest?" Jesus said to him:

" 'You shall love the Lord your God
with your whole heart,
with your whole soul,
and with all your mind.

This is the greatest and first commandment. The second is like it:

'You shall love your neighbor as yourself.'

On these two commandments the whole law is based, and the prophets as well."

6   From the holy gospel according to Mark   [101]
10:6-9*

Although the highest glory of married love is the begetting and full nurturing of offspring, husband and wife in their marriage grow into more mature levels of self-giving, of seeing life through the needs of the other, and of generous sacrifice for the well-being of every family member. This can only happen where there exists a total bonding of love—genuine fidelity—between husband and wife who "are no longer two, but one flesh" (Mt. 19:6).

Jesus said: "At the beginning of creation God made them male and female; for this reason a man shall leave his father and mother and the two shall become as one. They are no longer two but one flesh. Therefore let no man separate what God has joined."

7   From the holy gospel according to John   [102]
2:1-11*

In His desire to restore and elevate married life, Christ the Lord lavished the riches of His graces upon the love of husband and wife, even uniting it to His own divine love.

There was a wedding at Cana in Galilee, and the mother of Jesus was there. Jesus and his disciples had likewise been invited to the celebration. At a certain point the wine ran out, and Jesus' mother told him, "They have no more wine." Jesus replied, "Woman, how does this concern of yours involve me? My hour has not yet come." His mother instructed those waiting on table, "Do whatever he tells you." As prescribed for Jewish ceremonial washings, there were at hand six stone water jars, each one holding fifteen to twenty-five gallons. "Fill those jars with water," Jesus ordered, at which they filled them to the brim. "Now," he said, "draw some out and take it to the waiter in charge." They did as he instructed them. The waiter in charge tasted the water made wine, without knowing where it had come from; only the waiters knew, since they had drawn the water. Then the waiter in charge called the groom over and remarked to him: "People usually serve the choice wine first; then when the guests have been drinking a while, a lesser vintage. What you have done is keep the choice wine until now." Jesus performed this first of his signs at Cana in Galilee. Thus did he reveal his glory, and his disciples believed in him.

8   **From the holy gospel according to John**   [103]
    15:9-12*
    Firmly established by the Lord, the unity of marriage will radiate from the equal personal dignity of wife and husband, a dignity acknowledged by mutual and total love.

Jesus said to his disciples:
    "As the Father has loved me,
    so I have loved you.
    Live on in my love.
    You will live in my love
    if you keep my commandments,
    even as I have kept my Father's commandments,
    and live in his love.
    All this I tell you
    that my joy may be yours
    and your joy may be complete.
    This is my commandment:
    love one another
    as I have loved you.

9   **From the holy gospel according to John**   [104]
    15:12-16*
    The Savior of men and the Spouse of the Church comes into the lives of married Christians through the

sacrament of Matrimony. He abides with them thereafter
so that just as He loved the Church and handed Himself
over on her behalf, the spouses may love each other with
perpetual fidelity through mutual self-bestowal.

Jesus said to his disciples:

"This is my commandment:
love one another
as I have loved you.
There is no greater love than this:
to lay down one's life for one's friends.
You are my friends
if you do what I command you.
I no longer speak of you as slaves,
for a slave does not know what his master is about.
Instead, I call you friends,
since I have made known to you all that I heard from
   my Father.
It was not you who chose me,
it was I who chose you
to go forth and bear fruit.
Your fruit must endure,
so that all you ask the Father in my name
he will give you."

10   From the holy gospel according to John   [105]
17:20-26 or 17:20-23*

Following Christ who is the principle of life, by the
sacrifices and joys of their vocation and through their
faithful love, married people can become witnesses of the
mystery of love which the Lord revealed to the world by
His dying and His rising up to life again.

Long form follows; for short form omit what is in brackets.
Jesus looked up to heaven and prayed:

"Holy Father,
I do not pray for my disciples alone.

I pray also for those who will believe in me through
    their word,
that all may be one
as you, Father, are in me, and I in you;
I pray that they may be (one) in us,
that the world may believe that you sent me.
I have given them the glory you gave me
that they may be one, as we are one—
I living in them, you living in me—
that their unity may be complete.
So shall the world know that you sent me,
and that you loved them as you loved me.
[Father,
all those you gave me
I would have in my company
where I am,
to see this glory of mine
which is your gift to me,
because of the love you bore me before the world began.
Just Father,
the world has not known you,
but I have known you;
and these men have known that you sent me.
To them I have revealed your name,
and I will continue to reveal it
so that your love for me may live in them,
and I may live in them."]

OPENING PRAYER

1   [106]

Father,
you have made the bond of marriage
a holy mystery,
a symbol of Christ's love for his Church.

Hear our prayers for N. and N.
With faith in you and in each other
they pledge their love today.
May their lives always bear witness
to the reality of that love.

We ask you this
through our Lord Jesus Christ, your Son,
who lives and reigns with you and the Holy Spirit,
one God, for ever and ever.

2   [107]

Father,
hear our prayers for N. and N.,
who today are united in marriage before your altar.
Give them your blessing,
and strengthen their love for each other.

We ask you this
through our Lord...

3   [108]

Almighty God,
hear our prayers for N. and N.,
who have come here today
to be united in the sacrament of marriage.
Increase their faith in you and in each other,
and through them bless your Church
    (with Christian children).

We ask you this
through our Lord...

4   [109]

Father,
when you created mankind
you willed that man and wife should be one.
Bind N. and N.
in the loving union of marriage;

and make their love fruitful
so that they may be living witnesses
to your divine love in the world.

We ask you this
through our Lord....

BLESSING OF RINGS

1   [110]

Lord, bless these rings which we bless ✚ in your name.
Grant that those who wear them
may always have a deep faith in each other.
May they do your will
and always live together
in peace, good will, and love.

(We ask this) through Christ our Lord.

R. **Amen.**

2   [111]

Lord,
bless ✚ and consecrate N. and N.
in their love for each other.
May these rings be a symbol
of true faith in each other,
and always remind them of their love.

(We ask this) through Christ our Lord.

R. **Amen.**

PRAYERS OVER THE GIFTS

1   [112]

Lord,
accept our offering
for this newly-married couple, N. and N.

By your love and providence you have brought them
    together;
now bless them all the days of their married life.

(We ask this) through Christ our Lord.

2   [113]

Lord,
accept the gifts we offer you
on this happy day.
In your fatherly love
watch over and protect N. and N.,
whom you have united in marriage.

(We ask this) through Christ our Lord.

3   [114]

Lord,
hear our prayers
and accept the gifts we offer for N. and N.
Today you have made them one in the sacrament of
    marriage.
May the mystery of Christ's unselfish love,
which we celebrate in this eucharist,
increase their love for you and for each other.

(We ask this) through Christ our Lord.

PREFACES

1   [115]

Father, all-powerful and ever-living God,
we do well always and everywhere to give you thanks.
By this sacrament your grace unites man and woman
in an unbreakable bond of love and peace.

You have designed the chaste love of husband and wife
for the increase both of the human family
and of your own family born in baptism.

You are the loving Father of the world of nature;
you are the loving Father of the new creation of grace.
In Christian marriage you bring together the two orders
    of creation:
nature's gift of children enriches the world
and your grace enriches also your Church.

Through Christ the choirs of angels
and all the saints
praise and worship your glory.
May our voices blend with theirs
as we join in their unending hymn:

2   [116]

Father, all-powerful and ever-living God,
we do well always and everywhere to give you thanks
through Jesus Christ our Lord.

Through him you entered into a new covenant with your
    people.
You restored man to grace in the saving mystery of redemp-
    tion.
You gave him a share in the divine life
through his union with Christ.
You made him an heir of Christ's eternal glory.

This outpouring of love in the new covenant of grace
is symbolized in the marriage covenant
that seals the love of husband and wife
and reflects your divine plan of love.

And so, with the angels and all the saints in heaven
we proclaim your glory
and join in their unending hymn of praise:

3 [117]

Father, all-powerful and ever-living God,
we do well always and everywhere to give you thanks.

You created man in love to share your divine life.
We see his high destiny in the love of husband and wife,
which bears the imprint of your own divine love.

Love is man's origin,
love is his constant calling,
love is his fulfillment in heaven.

The love of man and woman
is made holy in the sacrament of marriage,
and becomes the mirror of your everlasting love.

Through Christ the choirs of angels
and all the saints
praise and worship your glory.
May our voices blend with theirs
as we join in their unending hymn:

HANC IGITUR [118]

The words in parentheses may be omitted if desired.

Father, accept this offering
from your whole family
and from N. and N., for whom we now pray.
You have brought them to their wedding day:
grant them (the gift and joy of children and)
a long and happy life together.

(Through Christ our Lord. Amen.)

NUPTIAL BLESSING

1 [119]

Father, by your power, *with the proper invitatory, as in no. 33
[p. 42].*

2   [120]

In the following prayer, either the paragraph *Holy Father, you created mankind,* or the paragraph *Father, to reveal the plan of your love,* may be omitted, keeping only the paragraph which corresponds to the reading of the Mass.

The priest faces the bride and bridegroom, and, with hands joined, says:

Let us pray to the Lord for N. and N.
who come to God's altar at the beginning of their married
    life
so that they may always be united in love for each other
(as now they share in the body and blood of Christ).

All pray silently for a short while. Then the priest extends his hands and continues:

Holy Father, you created mankind in your own image
and made man and woman to be joined as husband and wife
in union of body and heart
and so fulfill their mission in this world.

Father, to reveal the plan of your love,
you made the union of husband and wife
an image of the covenant between you and your people.
In the fulfillment of this sacrament,
the marriage of Christian man and woman
is a sign of the marriage between Christ and the Church.
Father, stretch out your hand, and bless N. and N.

Lord, grant that as they begin to live this sacrament
they may share with each other the gifts of your love
and become one in heart and mind
as witnesses to your presence in their marriage.
Help them to create a home together
(and give them children to be formed by the gospel
and to have a place in your family).

Give your blessings to N., your daughter,
so that she may be a good wife (and mother),
caring for the home,

faithful in love for her husband,
generous and kind.
Give your blessings to N., your son,
so that he may be a faithful husband
(and a good father).

Father, grant that as they come together to your table on earth,
so they may one day have the joy of sharing your feast in heaven.

(We ask this) through Christ our Lord.

R. **Amen.**

3 [121]

The priest faces the bride and bridegroom and, with hands joined, says:

My dear friends, let us ask God
for his continued blessings upon this bridegroom and his bride (or N. and N.).

All pray silently for a short while. Then the priest extends his hands and continues:

Holy Father, creator of the universe,
maker of man and woman in your own likeness,
source of blessing for married life,
we humbly pray to you for this woman
who today is united with her husband in this sacrament of marriage.

May your fullest blessing come upon her and her husband
so that they may together rejoice in your gift of married love
(and enrich your Church with their children).

Lord, may they both praise you when they are happy
and turn to you in their sorrows.
May they be glad that you help them in their work
and know that you are with them in their need.
May they pray to you in the community of the Church,
and be your witnesses in the world.

May they reach old age in the company of their friends,
and come at last to the kingdom of heaven.

(We ask this) through Christ our Lord.

R. **Amen.**

PRAYERS AFTER COMMUNION

1   [122]

Lord,
in your love
you have given us this eucharist
to unite us with one another and with you.
As you have made N. and N.
one in this sacrament of marriage
(and in the sharing of the one bread and the one cup),
so now make them one in love for each other.

(We ask this) through Christ our Lord.

2   [123]

Lord,
we who have shared the food of your table
pray for our friends N. and N.,
whom you have joined together in marriage.
Keep them close to you always.
May their love for each other
proclaim to all the world
their faith in you.

(We ask this) through Christ our Lord.

3   [124]

Almighty God,
may the sacrifice we have offered
and the eucharist we have shared
strengthen the love of N. and N.,
and give us all your fatherly aid.

(We ask this) through Christ our Lord.

BLESSING AT THE END OF MASS

1   [125]

God the eternal Father keep you in love with each other,
so that the peace of Christ may stay with you
and be always in your home.

R. **Amen.**

May (your children bless you,)
your friends console you
and all men live in peace with you.

R. **Amen.**

May you always bear witness to the love of God in this
    world
so that the afflicted and the needy
will find in you generous friends,
and welcome you into the joys of heaven.

R. **Amen.**

And may almighty God bless you all,
the Father, and the Son, ✙ and the Holy Spirit.

R. **Amen.**

2   [126]

May God, the almighty Father,
give you his joy
and bless you (in your children).

R. **Amen.**

May the only Son of God have mercy on you
and help you in good times and in bad.

R. **Amen.**

May the Holy Spirit of God
always fill your hearts with his love.

R. **Amen.**

And may almighty God bless you all,
the Father, and the Son, ✝ and the Holy Spirit.

R. **Amen.**

3   [127]

May the Lord Jesus, who was a guest at the wedding in
   Cana,
bless you and your families and friends.

R. **Amen.**

May Jesus, who loved his Church to the end,
always fill your hearts with his love.

R. **Amen.**

May he grant that, as you believe in his resurrection,
so you may wait for him in joy and hope.

R. **Amen.**

And may almighty God bless you all,
the Father, and the Son, ✝ and the Holy Spirit.

R. **Amen.**

PREPARING FOR
YOUR ANNIVERSARY

REFLECTIONS
LITURGICAL PRAYERS:
THE ANNIVERSARY
THE TWENTY-FIFTH ANNIVERSARY
THE FIFTIETH ANNIVERSARY

Soon, there will be a renewal of the marriage promises. *These words are marvelous, those pronounced by the couple in the rite of Matrimony as ministers of this sacrament:*

"I take you to be my wife (my husband). I promise to be true to you in good times and in bad, in sickness and in health. I will love you and honor you all the days of my life."

This promise, pronounced "in the name of the Father and the Son and the Holy Spirit," is at the same time a prayer addressed to God who is love—and who wishes to unite at the end all in the last alliance of the communion of saints.

At the moment in which you said these words, dear spouses, in different languages, in various places in the world, in different years, months and days, you administered the holy sacrament of your life, of your marriage, of your family:

the sacrament in which the love of God for man is reflected in the love of Christ for the Church.

Today you return with the heart and the mind—you return with faith, with hope and with love—to that great moment. And you renew in your souls that which made up the essential content of the sacrament of Matrimony. Its daily reality. You renew the alliance of man and woman! Before the God of alliance, you renew this alliance, penetrated by the gift of love. and the gift of life.

Pope John Paul II

tions. The husband and wife should confess and communicate on that day, and recommend to God, with a more than ordinary fervor, the happy progress of their marriage. They should renew their good purposes to sanctify it still more and more by mutual love and fidelity, and recover breath as it were, in our Lord, in order to support with more ease the burdens of their calling.''

One young bride wrote to her aunt: ''My marriage is wonderful—as a matter of fact, today is my 2-month anniversary. Lou and I get along very well. He's a good friend, as well as a good husband. It is a whole new life, and I enjoy being able to share it with the man I love. I have trouble cooking though. My mother spoiled me, always having dinner ready by the time I got home from work. I guess in time I'll learn... (Practice makes perfect).''

''Let Christian spouses not be discouraged by the difficulties they meet and let them not on this account abandon the Church,'' urges Pope Paul VI, ''but trusting in the strength of divine grace for which they must earnestly pray, rather than reducing divine law to the measure of their own will, let them rise to the height of the divine ideal and, renewing each day their good will, let them set out again cheerfully on their journey, whose destination is an eternity of life with God and whose reward here on earth is a deeper and more sanctifying love. 'Blessed are the clean of heart; they shall see God' (Matthew 5:8).''

Liturgical Prayers

THE ANNIVERSARIES OF MARRIAGE

On marriage anniversaries, especially the twenty-fifth and fiftieth anniversaries, the Mass of thanksgiving may be celebrated with the following prayers, if a votive Mass is permitted.

These prayers may also be used if desired at weekday Masses in ordinary time.

THE ANNIVERSARY

Opening Prayer

God our Father,
you created man and woman
to love each other
in the bond of marriage.
Bless and strengthen N. and N.
May their marriage become an increasingly more perfect sign
of the union between Christ and his Church.

We ask this through our Lord Jesus Christ, your Son,
who lives and reigns with you and the Holy Spirit,
one God, for ever and ever.

Prayer over the Gifts

Pray, brethren...

Father,
the blood and water that flowed

from the wounded heart of Christ your Son
was a sign of the mystery of our rebirth:
accept these gifts we offer in thanksgiving.
Continue to bless the marriage of N. and N.
with all your gifts.

Grant this in the name of Jesus the Lord.

Prayer after Communion

Let us pray.

Pause for silent prayer, if this has not preceded.

Lord,
you give us food and drink from heaven.
Bless N. and N. on their anniversary.
Let their love grow stronger
that they may find within themselves
a greater peace and joy.
Bless their home
that all who come to it in need
may find in it an example of goodness
and a source of comfort.
We ask this through Christ our Lord.

THE TWENTY-FIFTH
ANNIVERSARY OF MARRIAGE

Opening Prayer

Father,
you have blessed and sustained N. and N.
in the bond of marriage.
Continue to increase their love
throughout the joys and sorrows of life,
and help them to grow in holiness all their days.
Grant this through our Lord Jesus Christ, your Son,
who lives and reigns with you and the Holy Spirit,
one God, for ever and ever.

Prayer over the Gifts

Pray, brethren...

Father,

accept these gifts which we offer in thanksgiving for N.
    and N.

May they bring them continued peace and happiness.

We ask this through Christ our Lord.

Prayer after Communion

Let us pray.

Pause for silent prayer, if this has not preceded.

Father,

you bring N. and N. (and their children and friends) together
at the table of your family.

Help them grow in love and unity,

that they may rejoice together

in the wedding feast of heaven.

Grant this through Christ our Lord.

THE FIFTIETH ANNIVERSARY
OF MARRIAGE

Opening Prayer

God, our Father,

bless N. and N.

We thank you for their long and happy marriage

(for the children they have brought into the world)

and for all the good they have done.

As you blessed the love of their youth,

continue to bless their life together

with gifts of peace and joy.

We ask this through our Lord Jesus Christ, your Son,

who lives and reigns with you and the Holy Spirit,

one God, for ever and ever.

Prayer over the Gifts

Pray, brethren...
Lord,
accept the gifts we offer in thanksgiving for N. and N.
With trust in you and in each other
they have shared life together.
Hear their prayers,
and keep them in your peace.
We ask this through Christ our Lord.

Prayer after Communion

Let us pray.

Pause for silent prayer, if this has not preceded.

Lord,
as we gather at the table of your Son,
bless N. and N. on their wedding anniversary.
Watch over them in the coming years,
and after a long and happy life together
bring them to the feast of eternal life.
Grant this through Christ our Lord.

CHECKLISTS:

For the Wedding

Date of Wedding:_____ Time:_____

Place of Wedding: _____

Address: _____

Invitations:____formal / ____informal

_____no. of copies

Designed by _____

Printed by_____

Mailed by _____

_____ Map enclosed, with parking indicated

Sent to:

SAMPLE INVITATIONS

Formal

Mr. and Mrs. Ralph Smith
Mr. and Mrs. John F. Murphy
joyfully invite you to join them
in the celebration of the Nuptial Mass
at which their children
Eileen and Thomas
will confer upon each other
the Sacrament of Matrimony
Saturday, the second of May
nineteen hundred and eighty-two
at two o'clock
St. Jerome's Church
Stowe, Ohio
Reception
Parish Hall

Informal

Cecilia
and
Paul
will vow their lives
to one another
becoming one in Christ
during the Eucharistic Celebration
on Saturday, the twenty-fourth of June
nineteen hundred and eighty-three
Mr. and Mrs. Robert Grey
Mr. and Mrs. Stanley Myers
invite you to join them
to ask God's blessing
on this marriage
at eleven o'clock
St. Bridget's Church
Fort Wayne, Indiana
and at the festivities
following at Grant Park

Marriage license: _____

Marriage certificate: _____

Wedding ring: _____

Altar cloth and linens: _____

Wine: _____

Hosts: _____

Flowers: _____

Banner: _____

Candles for altar: _____

Wedding Booklets:

_____ no. of copies needed

Text permissions: _____

Music permissions (notes—lyrics): _____

Printed by: _____

or

To buy at: _____

Distributed by: _____

_____ at door;

_____ in pews after congregation is seated

_____ or: _____

Petitions for General Intercessions (Prayer of the Faithful)

prepared by:_____

Tape recording of the ceremony by: _____

Celebrant's vestment and stole: _____

If Concelebrants (their vestments and stoles): _____

_____

Deacon's vestment and stole_____

Bridal Dress _____

Dresses of Attendants_____

Gifts for:

Maid of Honor: _____

Best Man:_____

Bridesmaids: _____

Ushers:_____

Host:_____

Hostess: _____

For the Wedding Party

Priest-celebrant: _____

Concelebrants: _____

Deacon: _____

Server(s): _____

Readers: _____

_____

_____

Cantor(s): _____

Leader of Song: _____

Bride: _____

Parents of the Bride: _____

Groom: _____

Parents of Groom: _____

Witnesses: _____

   or

Maid of Honor: _____

Best Man: _____

Bridesmaids: _____

_____

_____

Ushers: _____

_____

_____

At the Church

Host: _____

Hostess: _____

Organist: _____

Permission to use organ: _____

Photographers (Professionals): _____

       When/where for Professionals: _____

_____

When/where for Amateurs: _____

_____ _____

For the Rehearsal

When: _____

Where: _____

Who: Wedding Party/Readers/Host/Hostess/

Organist and _____

For the Reception

Where: _____

When: _____

Decorations:_____

Flowers: _____

Banner:_____

Caterers: _____

Wedding Cake: _____

Other food: _____

_____

Beverages: _____

For the
Wedding Ceremony

INTRODUCTORY RITES

Entrance Song:

Title _____

Sung by_____
Choir   Congregation   Soloist

Procession of the Wedding Party to the Front
(one alternative)

1) Server(s) _____

2) Priest-celebrant _____

3) Maid of Honor_____

   Best Man _____

4) Bridesmaids and Ushers _____

_____

_____

5) Groom between his parents

6) Bride between her parents

Positions for Wedding Party (one alternative)

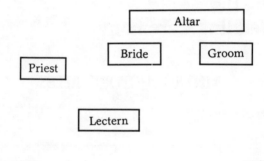

Bridesmaids
First pew: parents

Ushers
First pew: parents

GREETING:

____ by bride and groom

____ by priest-celebrant

PENITENTIAL RITE:

_____ A   _____ B   _____ C

GLORIA:

Sung by _____

Recited by _____

OPENING PRAYER:

_____ # 1 _____ # 2 _____ # 3 _____ # 4

Choose from pages 89-92.

LITURGY OF THE WORD

FIRST READING (from the Old Testament)

_____/by _____

Choose from pages 64-71.

RESPONSORIAL PSALM

_____/by _____

or sung by _____

Choose from pages 78-82.

SECOND READING (from the New Testament)

_____/by _____

Choose from pages 71-78.

ALLELUIA VERSE

_____/by _____

or sung by _____

Choose from pages 82-83.

GOSPEL

_____/by _____ celebrant

_____ deacon

Choose from pages 83-89.

Homily by _____

RITE FOR CELEBRATING MARRIAGE DURING MASS

Consent, and Blessing and Exchange of Rings, pages 59-61.

Profession of Faith if rubrics require it.

GENERAL INTERCESSIONS
(Prayer of the Faithful)

Beginning prayer by priest-celebrant or

deacon _____

Petition #1: _____

Petition #2: _____

Petition #3: _____

Petition #4: _____

Petition #5: _____

Petition #6: _____

Closing prayer by priest-celebrant _____

LITURGY OF THE EUCHARIST

PREPARATION OF THE ALTAR AND THE GIFTS

Offertory Procession:

Water: _____

Wine: _____

Hosts: _____

Other: _____

PRAYER OVER THE GIFTS # ___

Choose from pages 92-93.

PREFACE # ___

Choose from pages 93-95.

EUCHARISTIC PRAYER # ___

MEMORIAL ACCLAMATION:

Sung by _____

Recited by _____

COMMUNION RITE

LORD'S PRAYER

Sung by _____

Recited by congregation _____

NUPTIAL BLESSING: # ___

Choose from pages 95-98.

SIGN OF PEACE

BREAKING OF THE BREAD

COMMUNION

COMMUNION SONG:

Hymn: _____

Sung by: _____

PERIOD OF SILENCE
OR SONG OF PRAISE

PRAYER AFTER COMMUNION: # ____

Choose from page 98.

CONCLUDING RITE

Announcements (if any)

GREETING

BLESSING: # ____

Choose from pages 99-100.

DISMISSAL

Recessional Hymn: _____

Sung by: _____

Bride and groom lead the procession out of church.

ADDITIONAL CEREMONIES:

Homage to Blessed Virgin

When: _____

Where: _____

Other _____

  When: _____

  Where: _____

For the Anniversary

Date of Wedding Anniversary: _____

Date of Mass commemorating Anniversary: _____

Place of Anniversary Mass: _____

Address: _____

If a votive Mass is permitted:

  _____ Mass of Thanksgiving

  _____ Other

Special Opening Prayer, Prayer over the Gifts, Prayer after Communion, pages 107-111:

  _____ for the Anniversary

  _____ for the 25th Anniversary

  _____ for the 50th Anniversary

  With adaptation, the other checklists may be used according to your needs and plans.

NOTES

NOTES

CATECHESIS ON THE SACRAMENT OF MATRIMONY

CONTRACT AND SACRAMENT

What is marriage?

Marriage is the unbreakable union of man and woman. For non-Christians, it is the noblest of natural contracts; for Christians it is a sacrament—a sacred sign through which Christ gives His grace. This sacrament is also called Matrimony.

Why is marriage sometimes spoken of as a covenant?

Marriage is sometimes called a covenant because it is a lifelong commitment. St. Paul tells us that Christian marriage is a sacred sign that reflects the lasting covenant which unites Christ to His Church.

What is the purpose of marriage?

The purpose of marriage is twofold: unity and procreation, or the giving of love and the giving of life. The spouses commit themselves to loving, lifelong service—to one another and to the children whom God will send them.

Vatican II teaches: "Marriage and conjugal love are by their nature ordained toward the begetting and educating of children. Children are really the supreme gift of marriage and contribute very substantially to the welfare of their parents....

"Marriage to be sure is not instituted solely for procreation. Rather, its very nature as an unbreakable compact between persons, and the welfare of the children, both demand that the mutual love of the spouses be embodied in a rightly ordered manner, that it grow and ripen" (Church in the Modern World, no. 50).

When we speak of Christian marriage, another dimension must also be included: growth in holiness. The spouses help one another to become holier; moreover, children and parents reciprocally contribute to the sanctification of one another.

Why is marriage a sacrament?

Marriage is a sacrament because Jesus Christ chose to raise it to this level. As with three other sacraments, we do not know the precise occasion of institution, but both Scripture and Tradition manifest the sacramental nature of marriage.

For example, in St. Paul's Letter to the Ephesians (5:21-31), the Apostle compares Christian marriage to the permanent union of Christ and the Church. In this comparison St. Paul intimates that just as the union between Christ and His Church is a supernatural union which produces grace, so does the union produced by Matrimony confer grace on the husband and wife. So, he intimates that it is a sacrament, a grace-giving sign.

Another scriptural proof of the institution of Matrimony by Christ is His own emphasis on the permanence of marriage: "Therefore, let no man separate what God has joined" (Matthew 19:6). When the disciples heard this, they were amazed at their Master's difficult teaching, and from their surprise we can infer both that special grace from God is necessary to preserve the marriage union and that Jesus would never have taught such a demanding doctrine unless He had instituted the sacrament of Matrimony to provide us with all the necessary graces.

Finally, early Christian writings speak of marriage as something supernatural which of itself confers grace on the man and woman who receive it, and the Council of Trent formally defined that Matrimony is one of the seven sacraments.

How is the sacrament of Matrimony conferred?

Matrimony is conferred when a baptized man and a baptized woman express their mutual consent under conditions established or permitted by the Church. The bride and groom, therefore, confer the sacrament on one another.

In a mixed marriage, do the spouses receive the sacrament?

A mixed marriage is a valid, sacramental marriage for both spouses, if both have been validly baptized, have obtained the proper dispensation, and marry according to the other norms established by the Church. If one of the parties is not baptized, but the other necessary conditions (dispensation, etc.) have been fulfilled, the Catholic party—according to the opinion of some theologians—does receive the sacrament, but today most theologians would deny this. The non-Catholic, of course, could not, because Baptism is a pre-requisite to all the other sacraments.

Which are the effects of the sacrament of Matrimony?

The effects of the sacrament are: 1) an invisible bond that will last until the death of one of the spouses; and 2) the graces of the sacrament.

Which are the special graces of the sacrament of Matrimony?

When received in the state of grace, Matrimony increases sanctifying grace in the souls of the spouses. Every sacrament also gives to the recipient its own special grace, called sacramental grace. In Matrimony the sacramental grace brings to the couple the assurance of God's help to persevere together and grow in love, fidelity and holiness. Marriage is for life, and God who in His great wisdom knows the weakness of human nature (which, in spite of good-will, can cause friction in the best of marriages), provides through sacramental grace a constant source of strength for the couple. The sacramental grace of Matrimony includes the right to all the graces which are necessary to preserve mutual love in spite of anything and everything; the graces to face and overcome all difficulties, misunderstandings, sicknesses, or worries. The promise of graces which a couple receives in Matrimony does not last only for a year or two, but for an entire lifetime.

Anyone thinking of the great responsibilities of marriage and of the unforeseeable difficulties the future could hold might hesitate to enter into marriage. However, we must never forget God's role in the couple's life and His constant and infallible help, which is such an important and consoling aspect of the sacrament of Matrimony.

Are these graces of special importance today?

These graces are especially important today because there are many pressures and harmful influences in our society which make married life difficult and attempt to downgrade the importance of a strong family life.

Might one receive Matrimony without receiving all the effects?

Yes. It could happen that a person would receive the sacrament in a state of mortal sin. This would be a sacrilege, but the bond of Matrimony would be established nonetheless. With the restoration of grace (normally, through the sacrament of Penance), the graces of Matrimony would also be received.

Could it happen that one might go through the marriage ceremony according to the Church's norms, yet not be truly married?

This does happen, and therefore the Church sometimes grants decrees of nullity (annulments). A decree of nullity is a decision by a marriage tribunal that an apparently valid marriage was actually invalid from the beginning. The marriage would be invalid, for example, if one were forced into it or if one or both of the spouses married with the intention of never having children, or of breaking up the marriage if all did not go smoothly. Marriage must be undertaken as a free, irrevocable, lifelong commitment to one's spouse and to whatever children God may send.

RESPONSIBILITIES

Which are the chief duties of spouses to one another?

The chief duties of the spouses to one another are: 1) fidelity; 2) cohabitation; and 3) mutual assistance. Fidelity means that each partner in a marriage is bound to refrain from any activity proper only to marriage with any person other than the spouse. Cohabitation is a principle of the natural law which teaches that a husband and wife should live together and may separate temporarily and with mutual consent only for sufficiently important reasons, such as a temporary job transfer, etc. Mutual assistance includes mutual love and friendship and cooperation in regard to the financial support of the family. The normal way in which spouses help one another in the managing of the home is for the husband to work in order to receive a salary and the wife to take charge of household affairs and the care of the children, perhaps also supplementing the husband's income by holding a part-time job.

Which are the duties of parents toward their children?

The duties of a mother to her child begin as soon as she realizes she is pregnant, even if she is not absolutely certain, because at this time she must begin to abstain from anything that might injure the fetus—such as heavy work or strenuous exercise and the improper use of drugs and alcohol.

Once the child has been born, the parents have a grave obligation to have him baptized as soon as possible. From the time of the baby's birth to the point at which he or she is able to provide for himself, the parents have the obligation to provide for their child's physical, intellectual and spiritual needs. Providing for the physical needs of children includes giving them the proper and necessary food, clothing and shelter. Parents have the duty to see to it that their children receive all the necessary education, remembering that while formal education is useful and needed, the first real school is the family itself.

Important for the emotional growth of the children is the parents' avoidance of favoritism or the making of harmful comparisons.

Spiritual training of their children is also a duty of parents, who have the obligation to raise their offspring in such a way that their lives are directed always toward God, their Creator. Such spiritual training must include instructions on the truths of faith and morals, supervision and help in fulfilling religious and moral obligations, good advice and especially good example. Parents should send their children to Catholic schools whenever possible, and when this cannot be done they must provide adequate religious instruction for the children outside of school. Normally this will include regular attendance at parish CCD classes.

Are Catholic couples obliged to have as many children as possible?

No, Catholic couples are obliged only to act in a truly responsible manner in bringing children into the world and raising them well. This responsibility includes the recognition of the procreation of children as one of the fundamental purposes of marriage and the avoidance of abortion and artificial birth control, as contrary to God's law.

Why are abortion and the use of artificial means of birth control seriously sinful?

Abortion and contraception are seriously sinful because they are against both the natural and the divine law. Artificial birth control is evil because it frustrates the natural activity of the body which God has ordained for the procreation of children. Direct abortion, the intentional killing of the fetus, is murder and can never be permitted.

What is indirect abortion?

Indirect abortion occurs when the fetus dies as a result of an operation performed on the mother. Indirect abortion is not sinful if the death of the fetus was not intended, but only tolerated out of necessity in order to save at least the life of the mother. Such an operation resulting in the death of the fetus is permitted only when it is certain that without the operation both mother and child would die. The fetus must always be baptized.

Are there methods of birth control that do not offend God?

Yes, there are natural methods of birth control which do not offend God if used for right reasons and on a temporary basis.

What is Natural Family Planning?

Natural Family Planning is a name given to certain methods which are in accord with the harmonies which the Creator has impressed upon human nature. It uses no chemicals and no gadgets. It is based on sound scientific knowledge. It is completely harmless, reliable and healthful.

Is Natural Family Planning morally and religiously acceptable?

Natural Family Planning, rightly used, is both religiously and morally acceptable, because it accords with what both reason and revelation say about human nature and human sexuality.

Why do we say "rightly used"?

We say "rightly used," because:

—it requires use of intelligence and self-control;

—it should be used only when married people have serious motives for spacing out births.

What might create serious reasons for spacing out births?

Some serious reasons for spacing out births can derive from the physical or psychological conditions of husband or wife, or from external conditions. Selfishness, however, is a *sinful* motive.

Is a marriage rendered invalid by childlessness?

A truly valid marriage is not rendered invalid by circumstances that develop later. Therefore, if a couple married with the intention of accepting the children God would send them, childlessness would not render their marriage invalid. Vatican II teaches: "Marriage persists as a whole manner and communion of life, and maintains its value and indissolubility, even when, despite the often intense desire of the couple, offspring are lacking" (*Church in the Modern World,* no. 50).

Which are the chief characteristics of marriage?

The chief characteristics of marriage are unity and indissolubility. These characteristics apply to *all* marriages, whether sacramental or not. They are rooted in the law of God. Marriage must join one man and one woman for life.

Fallen human nature is weak in this regard. In fact, even God's chosen people were permitted to relax their standards. The sacrament of Matrimony was instituted to help couples maintain the unity and fidelity which the divine law imposes. Jesus explained that He was re-establishing the original order willed by God:

"Then some Pharisees came up and as a test began to ask him whether it was permissible for a husband to divorce his wife. In reply he said, 'What command did Moses give you?' They answered, 'Moses permitted divorce and the writing of a decree of divorce.' But Jesus told them: 'He wrote that commandment for you because of your stubbornness. At the beginning of creation God made them male and female; for this reason a man shall leave his father and mother and the two shall become as one. They are no longer two but one flesh. Therefore let no man separate what God has joined.' Back in the house again, the disciples began to question him about this. He told them, 'Whoever divorces his wife and marries another commits adultery against her; and the woman who divorces her husband and marries another commits adultery' " (Mark 10:2-12).°

°In his weekly general audiences from September 5, 1979 to April 2, 1980, Pope John Paul II commented in detail on the unity and indissolubility of marriage in the light of this passage from Mark and its counterpart in Matthew 19:3-9 with its reference to Genesis (chapters 1 and 2). These talks have been compiled and indexed in a handy volume, entitled *Original Unity of Man and Woman*—Catechesis on the Book of Genesis (Boston: St. Paul Editions. 1981). (Available from addresses at the end of this book; also inquire about the volume of subsequent addresses at the weekly general audiences:

Is the indissolubility of marriage beneficial?

Definitely. Among the advantages of this unbreakable oneness are:

—the security that husband and wife enjoy;

—mutual fidelity and mutual help;

—domestic and social peace and order;

—the procreation of children and their good upbringing.

Is divorce ever permissible?

If by divorce, we mean the dissolving of a valid marriage, this can almost never be done.°° Normally the marriage bond is dissolved only by the death of one of the spouses.

But if we mean by "divorce" the civil process by which the *state* "dissolves" a marriage, the Church does permit such a procedure when a couple has a serious reason for separating. Neither of the spouses is free to remarry, however, for in the eyes of God and of the Church they have only separated; they are still married to one another.

Catechesis on the Sermon on the Mount entitled: *Blessed Are the Pure of Heart,* in which His Holiness treats such topics as love and lust, adultery, concupiscence, purity of heart, pornography, etc.).

°°There are two rare cases in which the Church allows a valid marriage to be dissolved. The first is the "pauline privilege." This teaching is based on 1 Corinthians 7:12-17 and concerns the relationship between two un-baptized persons who have married and even consummated their marriage. If one of these spouses is later baptized, and the other spouse is opposed to Christianity and no longer consents to live with the Christian spouse or poses a threat to the Christian's faith or moral life, the marriage may be dissolved. The Christian spouse is then free to remarry. The second case in which a marriage may be dissolved is when a marriage between baptized persons or between a baptized person and one not baptized has not been consummated by the marriage act. For serious reasons and under certain conditions such a non-consummated marriage may be dissolved by a dispensation from the Holy Father or by the profession of solemn vows in a religious order of one of the persons.

What are some reasons for the Church to grant permission to separate?

The reason for *perpetual* separation arises from adultery of one of the partners. Other causes which permit the injured partner to seek a *temporary or indefinite* separation are: criminal or shameful conduct, the education of the children in schism or heresy, grave danger to soul and body. A priest should be consulted, normally.

Did Jesus make an exception to the law of indissolubility?

In Matthew 19:9, we find the so-called *porneia* clause, which has been variously translated: "except for unchastity" (RSV), "lewd conduct is a separate case" (NAB), "I am not speaking of fornication" (JB), and also variously understood. Whatever the phrase's meaning, however, theologians are agreed that Jesus was not making an exception. In the parallel passages—Mark 10:11ff., and Luke 16:18—we find no exception. Another source to be consulted is 1 Corinthians 7:10-11.

Scripture is a harmonious whole and does not contradict itself. Hence the *porneia* clause has to be regarded as in accord with the rest of New Testament teaching.

Is a climate of divorce harmful to Christian marriage?

Such a climate is very harmful. The ease with which a man or woman can obtain a civil divorce constitutes an ever-present threat which fosters insecurity, instability, infidelity and the limitation of offspring. When a civil divorce has actually been obtained, the children suffer, torn between conflicting loyalties, are neglected, and even rejected. Their unhappiness, in turn, fosters alcoholism, drug addiction, crime and other social disorders. A society which permits easy divorce is tending toward its own destruction.

What are some needs of today's divorced Catholics?

Today's divorced Catholic needs:

—special guidance not to become bitter, not to talk about "rules of the Church," when these are the rules of Christ;

—guidance in keeping with the eternal teachings of Christ to overcome feelings of loneliness and desolation;

—encouragement to keep close to the sacraments, especially Holy Communion;

—encouragement never to enter into an invalid marriage, because that cuts one off from receiving the life-giving and life-sustaining sacraments.

What is recommended for a Catholic living in an invalid marriage?

For a Catholic living in an invalid marriage, the religious problems are greater and the need for counseling is also greater. Such Catholics must never lose hope or lose sight of salvation. They should by all means remain faithful to Sunday Mass, parish life and personal prayer. It is a difficult way to live and reach salvation—but the mercy of God is great, especially to the contrite heart. °

° *Remarried Divorcees and Eucharistic Communion,* by Rev. Bertrand de Margerie, S.J. (Boston: St. Paul Editions, 1980). (Available from addresses at the back of this book.)

PREPARATION

Does everyone have a right to marry?

The Church has always considered marriage as a natural right. However, she wisely asks that Catholics not exercise this right until they have reached sufficient psychological maturity. In our time and culture such maturity is generally not achieved until young persons have entered their twenties.

What does psychological maturity involve?

Such maturity involves an *understanding* that marriage is a lifelong, total commitment between a man and woman ordered to mutual love and help and the procreation and education of children, coupled with a realistic *awareness* of the types of difficulties to be encountered and the means of coping with them. It also involves *freedom and firmness of will*—freedom from outside pressures and true willingness to commit oneself to a life of loving service.

A person is psychologically *immature* if he repeatedly wavers in his opinions and convictions, is childish in his attitudes and viewpoints, and lacks emotional control. Someone who shows such immaturity should be advised to seek help in growing toward maturity before facing the serious commitment of marriage.

What are the "marriage banns"?

The marriage banns are public announcements of an intended marriage made in the parish churches of both the man and woman on three consecutive Sundays or holy days of obligation. The purpose of the banns is to discover any impediments which might exist and to avoid secret marriages. If a person knows of an impediment to a planned marriage, he is bound in conscience to make it known to the pastor or another of the priests involved.

By her practice of announcing the marriage banns, the Church demonstrates her special concern that every marriage may be a valid and holy one.

Which are some of the impediments to Christian marriage?

There are two different types of impediments: diriment and prohibitive. Diriment impediments make an attempted marriage invalid, unless (when possible) a dispensation is obtained. In other words, if a couple were to go through with a marriage ceremony in spite of these obstacles there would be no marriage.

Some diriment impediments are: lack of age (a boy must be at least sixteen and a girl fourteen); close blood relationship, as between second cousins or nearer relatives; close blood relationship of a party's prospective spouse with the same party's deceased spouse; difference of worship (one party is not baptized); clerical state (one party is a priest or deacon); solemn religious vows binding one or both parties.

Prohibiting impediments, which forbid marriage and make it unlawful but do not in any way affect its validity, include: 1) certain simple vows, such as the vow of chastity, and 2) mixed religion (a baptized Catholic marrying a baptized non-Catholic). As with some diriment impediments, dispensations may be granted in certain circumstances.

What should preparation for Christian marriage include?

A couple preparing for Matrimony should pray for God's help and direction and study the beauty, nobility and duties of the married life. They should practice virtue, especially chastity, and ask the advice of those who can be of great help to them, particularly their parents and the priest to whom they usually go to confession. Frequent reception of the sacraments of Penance and Holy Eucharist will also bring the grace which is needed to prepare for and begin their married life. The couple should also attend the Pre-Cana or similar courses offered by their diocese, which provide valuable helps and instruction in preparation for the sacrament.

What is necessary for the worthy reception of Matrimony?

To receive the sacrament worthily, it is necessary to be in the state of grace (that is, free from mortal sin), to know and understand the duties of married life, and to obey the laws of the Church concerning marriage.

How does the marriage of a Catholic take place?

Normally the marriage of a Catholic takes place in the presence of a priest (or deacon) and two witnesses.° The sacrament is conferred by each spouse on the other when they express their mutual consent to the marriage, promising lifelong fidelity. These promises may be stated by the spouses (there are two formulas approved for use in the United States), or else the bride and groom may individually respond "I do" to the questions asked by the person officiating.

What is the role of the state concerning Matrimony?

Marriage is by its nature a social institution, and so it is necessary that it come under the authority of society's laws. Marriages of the unbaptized are in fact entirely under the authority of the state, because the state has power to govern in areas where only the natural law is concerned. However, the case of Chris-

---

°For sufficiently weighty reasons, the Church may grant a dispensation allowing a Catholic to be married before a non-Catholic minister or even a civil official. Also, when no priest or deacon will be available for a month (as in mission territories) a man and woman may marry in the presence of two witnesses and then have the marriage registered in Church records. When someone is at the point of death, and no competent priest is available, he or she may marry before two witnesses. (This might be done, for example, to rectify a common-law marriage, if neither spouse were bound by a previous marriage bond.)

local bishop could grant a dispensation and permit the marriage to take place before a minister or even a civil official.

A Catholic priest (or deacon) and a non-Catholic minister may not officiate together at a mixed marriage, each performing his respective rite. The Church also forbids that another religious ceremony be held either before or after the Catholic ceremony.

A Catholic and an Orthodox marry validly if any sacred minister is present; for such a marriage to be lawful, however, two dispensations are necessary— one from the impediment of mixed religion and the other from the obligation of marrying before a priest (deacon) and two witnesses. °

Bishops and parish priests should have special care for the spiritual welfare of the Catholic spouse and the children of a mixed marriage, and should foster unity between the husband and wife.

°Documents on mixed marriages may be obtained from the addresses at the back of this book: *Instruction on Mixed Marriages* (Matrimonii Sacramentum) issued by the Sacred Congregation for the Doctrine of the Faith on March 18, 1966; *Apostolic Letter on Mixed Marriages* (Matrimonia Mixta) issued by Pope Paul VI on March 31, 1970—effective October 1, 1970; and *Statement on the Implementation of the Apostolic Letter on Mixed Marriages* of the National Conference of Catholic Bishops (U.S.A.), issued January 1, 1971.

SECRETS FOR
A SUCCESSFUL MARRIAGE

TO THE YOUNG WIFE

1. Be good, and by means of prayer and the spirit of sacrifice, strive to overcome your faults in order to make your husband's life more pleasant.

2. Do not do all the talking, but remember your husband would appreciate you listening to him, too.

3. Lovingly prepare good meals, and keep everything in the house neat and attractive, including yourself.

4. Avoid jealousy. Have faith in your husband, not expecting that he repeat the words: "I love you" a thousand times a day; instead, forget your own sensitiveness and anticipate his desires.

5. Strive to understand your husband so that he will not feel alone with his problems. With your moral energy and with your prayer sustain him in his moments of depression.

6. Be patient with your husband's defects, and occasionally praise his good qualities. Be humble enough to admit your own failings without blaming him. When you are wrong be able to say: "I am sorry."

7. Do not give all your thoughts to clothes, possessions and entertainment, since your first duty is to please your husband, not yourself.

8. Reserve all your intimacies and affections for your husband, and with others be friendly but modest and reserved.

9. Do not amuse yourself by gossiping about your neighbors, or listening to others' complaints about their husbands and families.

10. Consider yourself "queen" of your home, and look after the well-being of your family. Assure the peaceful serenity of your new life while awaiting the children that God will send you to multiply your happiness.

TO THE YOUNG HUSBAND

1. Show your wife the same courtesy you showed her on the day of your wedding.

2. Have the greatest respect for her personality and permit her to preserve rightful affection toward her parents and her former home.

3. Permit her to have good, elevated thoughts, even if they do not always agree with your own, especially if they deal with the things of God.

4. Honor her motherhood.

5. Confide in her, and, with your love for her, inspire her to confide in you, so that you will be able to comfort and guide one another.

6. Show yourself—and truly be—happy to stay in her company. Devote to her as much of your time as possible. Let her be your companion wherever you go.

7. Show her that, for your family, you serenely and joyfully sacrifice your personal comfort and gladly do as much work as possible.

8. Appreciate her work and her love. When you see her tired, do not feel it beneath you to give her a hand.

9. Welcome and ask for her opinion and advice, happy if you can benefit from her experience to make a better decision.

10. Remember that when there is a disturbance in the family, you must not immediately blame her for it. Once your anger has passed, examine where the fault lies and if it is yours, acknowledge it and be able to say "I am sorry." If the fault is hers, tell her kindly but also, if necessary, with firmness.

TO PARENTS

What do young people most want their parents to do for them—or not to do? A world-wide survey of nearly one hundred thousand boys and girls in Europe, North and South America, Australia and India came up with ten *do's* and *don'ts.*

1. Treat all your children with equal affection.
2. Keep close to them.
3. Make their friends welcome in your home.
4. Don't quarrel in front of them.
5. Be thoughtful to each other.
6. Never lie to them.
7. Always answer their questions.
8. Don't punish them in the presence of others.
9. Be constant in your affection and moods.
10. Concentrate on good points, not failings.

BUILDING
YOUR FAMILY LIBRARY

Books, magazines and pamphlets are available from any of the addresses at the back of this book.

Fostering the Nobility of Marriage and the Family

This pamphlet is an excerpt from the Second Vatican Council's document, "Pastoral Constitution on the Church in the Modern World." 16 pages — PM0780

Growing Up

M. Josephine Colville

Rhymes to help in the guidance of young children, all based on real happenings.
"Having a heart for others
Means that yours must be a prize.
No matter how you're little,
There's no telling of its size."
168 pages — MS0264

Lifetime of Love

S. L. Hart

The practical problems of everyday family living. Backed by the sound doctrine of Vatican II. Covers the whole span of married life—from the day of the wedding until "sunset." Newlyweds, inlaws, the budget, raising children, sex instruction for little ones, divorce, birth control, family cooperation, the role of mother and father, teenagers, growing old together—these and countless more topics in this complete up-to-date marriage manual. 534 pages — MS0350

Yes to Life

Edited by Daughters of St. Paul

An invaluable source-book bringing together the consistent teaching of the Church through the centuries on the sacredness of human life.

Here in one volume is proclaimed the fundamental truth of the value of all human life in the words of the Fathers of the Church, the Popes, Vatican II and the bishops of our day. 330 pages — EP1110

Looking Ahead to Marriage

Daughters of St. Paul

From the most sublime to the most practical, "Looking Ahead to Marriage" delves into the meaning of the marriage commitment. Comprehensive material on every aspect of engagement and married life itself. Partial contents: Love, what is it?; Premarital chastity; parental advice or opposition; emotions; sacramental grace; the Church's teaching on birth control; working mothers; communicating; sharing. 336 pages — CA0120

Teenagers and Purity—Teenagers and Going Steady—Teenagers Looking Toward Marriage

Rev. Robert J. Fox

Based on the Vatican's "Declaration on Sexual Ethics," this booklet is a simple but valuable presentation of the Catholic outlook on sexuality. It is directed to teenagers in a style that is at once clear and encouraging, informative and uplifting. 62 pages — MS0660

Successful Parenting

Ann M. and John F. Murphy

An optimistic book on the challenging role of today's parent. 200 pages — MS0657

Teenagers Today

A friend of youth

A most popular book with teens today, since it answers all that they ask about—popularity, dating, spirituality, etc. 168 pages — MS0665

Woman: Her Influence and Zeal

Rev. James Alberione, SSP, STD

Father Alberione sets forth precisely what the Christian woman should be—regardless of her age or station. 316 pages — MS0820

Your Right To Be Informed

Daughters of St. Paul

Directed to the teenager, this book also finds many parents and other adults among its readers! Relevant, complete development of topics such as God, man, life of Christ, temperaments, conscience, morals—in simple, clear language. Its positive and optimistic approach to life is irresistible. 432 pages— CA0090

The Family—Center of Love and Life

Pope Paul VI, Pope John Paul I, Pope John Paul II

These messages regarding family life in the modern world reflect the particular role which the family is called to play in the entire plan of salvation. 361 pages — EP0484

"You Are the Future, You Are My Hope"

Pope John Paul II
Compiled and indexed by the Daughters of St. Paul
Volume one of talks of His Holiness *to young people* of all ages. Reveals the stirring personal appeal of the Pope to the new generation. Excellent for youth and those involved in guidance. 326 pages; 16 pages of full-color photos — EP1120

I Believe in Youth, Christ Believes in Youth

Pope John Paul II
Compiled and indexed by the Daughters of St. Paul
A second volume of the Pope's talks to youth.
304 pages — EP0586

Basic Catechism

Daughters of St. Paul
This concise, direct book presents the fundamentals of the Catholic Faith in a question-and-answer format with related scriptural quotations.

Thoroughly indexed for ready reference, it is a vital handbook for anyone desiring to deepen or clarify his belief. 208 pages — RA0007

The Family Catechism

Daughters of St. Paul
Almost nine hundred questions and answers on our Faith: truths, moral teachings, sacraments and prayer, with two special sections on the family. New and up-to-date, brief, clear and scriptural. The only book of its kind. For teenagers and adults. With index. 300 pages.

The Role of the Christian Family in the Modern World *(Familiaris consortio)*
Pope John Paul II. — EP0973

**Natural Family Planning—
the 100% Solution**
Father Herbert F. Smith, S.G.; Dr. Joseph M. Gambescia, M.D. and Albert Vera. — PM1315

The Bible for Everyone
Daughters of St. Paul
A complete Bible history, offering black and white art masters throughout. For individual or group study, for teens and adults, the entire Bible vividly unfolds—a marvelous introduction to the Scriptures. — SC0020

Subscriptions *

The Family—published monthly and bi-monthly (July-August). It contains:

—Spiritually enriching features for every member of the family
—Intriguing lives of saints
—Optimistic spotlights on the world
—Articles on Scripture
—Response to readers' religious or moral questions
—Thoughts of the Pope

---

*Write for subscription information for *The Family, My Friend* and *Strain Forward* to any of the addresses at the back of this book.

—Psychology from a practical Christian viewpoint

—Religious education for children and the family

—Contemporary prayers, inspirational verses, page for young people, movie reviews, photo album, and much, much more!

My Friend*

The ideal magazine for children!

For ages 6-12; 32 pages of fun and learning.

Bible stories; Beautiful lives of the saints; Contests; Projects; Science; Many other features which will keep children involved; Comes out every month (except July and August).

Strain Forward*

The magazine with depth! An excellent help for deepening the spiritual life. Published monthly, except bi-monthly (July-August), Strain Forward contains:

—Sunday Liturgy Themes

—Talks of the Pope to bishops, priests, religious, seminarians and all the People of God

—Thoughts and reflections for spiritual growth.

---

*Please see footnote about subscribing on p. 161.

Daughters of St. Paul

IN MASSACHUSETTS
50 St. Paul's Ave., Jamaica Plain, Boston, MA 02130;
617-522-8911; 617-522-0875.
172 Tremont Street, Boston, MA 02111; 617-426-5464;
617-426-4230.

IN NEW YORK
78 Fort Place, Staten Island, NY 10301; 212-447-5071; 212-447-5086.
59 East 43rd Street, New York, NY 10017; 212-986-7580.
625 East 187th Street, Bronx, NY 10458; 212-584-0440.
525 Main Street, Buffalo, NY 14203; 716-847-6044.

IN NEW JERSEY
Hudson Mall — Route 440 and Communipaw Ave.,
Jersey City, NJ 07304; 201-433-7740.

IN CONNECTICUT
202 Fairfield Ave., Bridgeport, CT 06604; 203-335-9913.

IN OHIO
2105 Ontario Street (at Prospect Ave.), Cleveland, OH 44115;
216-621-9427.
25 E. Eighth Street, Cincinnati, OH 45202; 513-721-4838;
513-421-5733.

IN PENNSYLVANIA
1719 Chestnut Street, Philadelphia, PA 19103; 215-568-2638.

IN VIRGINIA
1025 King Street, Alexandria, VA 22314; 703-683-1741;
703-549-3806.

IN FLORIDA
2700 Biscayne Blvd., Miami, FL 33137; 305-573-1618.

IN LOUISIANA
4403 Veterans Memorial Blvd., Metairie, LA 70002; 504-887-7631;
504-887-0113.
1800 South Acadian Thruway, P.O. Box 2028, Baton Rouge, LA 70821;
504-343-4057; 504-381-9485.

IN MISSOURI
1001 Pine Street (at North 10th), St. Louis, MO 63101; 314-621-0346;
314-231-1034.

IN ILLINOIS
172 North Michigan Ave., Chicago, IL 60601; 312-346-4228;
312-346-3240.

IN TEXAS
114 Main Plaza, San Antonio, TX 78205; 512-224-8101.

IN CALIFORNIA
1570 Fifth Ave., San Diego, CA 92101; 619-232-1442.
46 Geary Street, San Francisco, CA 94108; 415-781-5180.

IN HAWAII
1143 Bishop Street, Honolulu, HI 96813; 808-521-2731.

IN ALASKA
750 West 5th Ave., Anchorage, AK 99501; 907-272-8183.

IN CANADA
3022 Dufferin Street, Toronto 395, Ontario, Canada.

IN ENGLAND
128, Notting Hill Gate, London W11 3QG, England.
133 Corporation Street, Birmingham B4 6PH, England.
5A-7 Royal Exchange Square, Glasgow G1 3AH, England.
82 Bold Street, Liverpool L1 4HR, England.

IN AUSTRALIA
58 Abbotsford Rd., Homebush, N.S.W. 2140, Australia